HOW TO BE YOUR BEST

WHEN YOU ARE FEELING YOUR WORST

DIEGO MESA

HOW TO BE YOUR BEST
ISBN: 978-1-949106-04-6
Copyright © 2018 Diego Mesa

Published by Word and Spirit Publishing.
P.O. Box 701403
Tulsa, Oklahoma 74170
wordandspiritpublishing.com

CONTENTS

FOREWORD

Someone once said, "It's not what happens to us that causes us to be successful, but what happens through us. Our reaction and response to what happens is what makes the difference." We will either be a thermometer that reacts to the temperature or a thermostat that controls the temperature. Let me come right out and say, *hard and difficult things are going to happen to all of us. That's life!* Like losing a job, income, retirement investments, or, God forbid, a loved one. It may be that we fall short in accomplishing our goals and ambitions. Our dreams may not be fulfilled, our health and marriage may fall by the wayside, or we may fail to keep our promises and commitments. Yet none of this means that we are a failure.

Failure is a mindset. It is the way we view the events of life. We, like Jesus, are going to be put in situations and scenarios where we may not feel our best. *We must refuse to allow it to control our performance and the outcome in our lives. We must not let it be an excuse to be less or do less than expected.* We can learn and grow from our life experiences when our perception, insight, and awareness change.

Everyday life is about choices. Doing your best or your worst is also a choice. In reality, anyone can do what is right or expected in perfect or favorable conditions. It's doing the right thing during difficult times that makes all the difference in the world, and that's when we shine the brightest.

Doing good and being your best in spite of hard times, doesn't happen accidentally, but intentionally. It's not something you inherit, but something you learn and develop. Everyone is capable of mastering these skills, but for them to be effective, we must be disciplined and consistent. Implementing them sporadically won't get it done. Instead, we should strive to be an example of good all the time; in every place, and with everyone.

And in all things show yourself to be an example of good works, with purity in doctrine [having the strictest regard for integrity and truth], dignified, sound and beyond reproach in instruction, so that the opponent [of the faith] will be shamed, having nothing bad to say about us.

—Titus 2:7-8 AMP

Great athletes, who master their gift, have the capability of playing through the pain and staying on track because of who they are and what they want to become. They can adjust quickly without penalty, in spite of their opponent; they learn to call an audible without getting flustered, and keep on playing the game. God has given us His amazing grace to help us be our best when feeling our worst, and to do good when we really feel bad.

This book is dedicated to Jesus who endured the uncomfortable, unexpected, and unwanted events in His life and ministry. He shows us *how to give our best when the worst is happening all around us*. It is my prayer that you will take this journey with me because of who you are and what you want to become.

—Diego Mesa

CHAPTER 1

The word which God sent to the children of Israel, preaching peace through Jesus Christ—He is Lord of all—that word you know, which was proclaimed throughout all Judea, and began from Galilee after the baptism which John preached: how God anointed Jesus of Nazareth with the Holy Spirit and with power, who went about doing good and healing all who were oppressed by the devil, for God was with Him.

—Acts 10:36-38

It's an innocent little question that most of us ask—or hear— several times a day: *How are you doing?* But that simple little question can get pretty tricky. Maybe you walk around feeling good every day and giving your very best all the time. But the reality is that most of us are facing a challenge in at least one area of our lives—if not more. We may wonder, *Are they asking a question about how I am feeling right now? Or are they asking about the condition of my attitude and what is going on in my life? Do they* really *want to know how I'm doing, or are they just being polite? Do I answer truthfully or just smile and say, "fine?"* I want to challenge you, in the moments when you feel your very worst—that's when God wants you to give your very best.

Jesus was able to turn the tide on the devil's plots, plans, and strategies by *doing good.* In this passage of scripture in the book of Acts, three things stand out: first, Jesus did good because he had the *Holy Spirit* and *power that was available and accessible to Him.* Second, Jesus did good by bringing *healing to all who were oppressed by the devil,* in action and demonstration to do good. And third, Jesus did good because *God was with Him, a partnership of unity and purpose to do good.*

Oftentimes, we think that Jesus can't possibility know about or understand the things we go through. We think He is unable to identify with our emotions, because we believe He was isolated and insulated from the conditions of the world; or we perceive that He had the perfect life and never experienced frustrations or disappointment. But in Hebrews it says, "For we do not have a High Priest who is unable to sympathize and understand our weaknesses and temptations, but One who has been tempted [knowing exactly how it feels to be human] in every respect as we are, yet without [committing any] sin," (Hebrews 4:15 AMP). This verse tells us that Jesus knows *exactly* how it feels to be human. He *understands our weaknesses and temptations.* Jesus experienced every emotion of failure, defeat, and loss that we do. In the Message Bible it says, *"He experienced it all!"*

CHAPTER 1

I sometimes wonder if Jesus ever felt like quitting or giving up. I wonder if He ever felt like screaming out in frustration. I wonder if He felt worn out, stressed out, or just simply not at His best. I wonder if He ever felt like doing nothing, just being selfish. I wonder whether Jesus had a stress ball in His robe or whether He ever made Himself stop and count to 10. He was 100 percent God, and 100 percent man, with human emotions and feelings. He experienced it all. Did Jesus ever feel like a five, but give a ten? Did He ever smile when He felt like frowning? Did He ever talk, preach, and teach when He felt like saying nothing?

Amazingly, throughout Jesus' life journey—with all of its expectations, demands, criticisms, judgments, ridicules, betrayals, brutality, abandonment, disappointments, and hopelessness—He did what we all should strive to do—*be our best* and *do good*. There is an important lesson here that we need to learn.

Triumphing Heroes

We love our sports heroes—especially those who triumph in the face of adversity. There are many examples of famous athletes who performed well while they were injured. During the 1997 NBA Championship Finals, Michael Jordan had the flu—but he still managed to walk out on the court and score 38 points to bring Chicago a win.

In 2004, Curt Schilling pitched for the Boston Red Sox game in the ALCS, despite a horrific ankle injury that had required last-minute surgery. Schilling only gave up one run in seven innings, with the blood soaking through his sock plainly visible. He played an important role in helping Boston go on to win their first World Series title in 86 years and his heroic efforts earned him a place of honor in Red Sox lore.

In the 1990 NBA Finals, Willis Reed of the New York Knicks walked on the court to play with a torn muscle in his right leg. In the 1988 World Series, Kirk Gibson hit an amazing walk-off home run, while he hobbled with injuries in both legs. In 2008, Tiger Woods won the U.S. Open Championship playing with a torn ACL and two stress fractures of the tibia. And in the 1996 Olympics, gymnast Kerri Strug landed her second vault on her feet to clinch the gold medal for the U.S., although she had suffered a third-degree lateral sprain and tendon damage on her first attempt.

We think of these athletes as heroes because they performed—even excelled—despite how they felt. The story behind these athletes goes beyond physical injury or pain. They were able to push beyond the pain and tap into a threshold—bypassing the normal emotional response. Most people perform according to how they feel. If they're feeling good they perform well, but if they're feeling bad, it's a different story. Everyone can feel painful effects at deep levels, but we must learn to push beyond our pain threshold and still do our best.

If we're struggling in our marriage; if we're struggling with our health; if we're struggling in our finances, we must recognize that the physical and emotional parts of us are deeply connected. It's important that we care for the whole body. If not, the results will affect our overall performance.

Emotional stability should be our number one priority. Believers often start off well, but then because of circumstances they stop going to church; they stop praying; *and they stop tithing.* They just stop doing the Christian life. They stop being nice or kind to people. They just stop—like an abandoned car falling off a cliff and left there to corrode, never to be used or driven again. People let their pain and discomfort determine their commitment, their motivation, and their effort in what they do.

On many occasions, I have run into people and asked them, "I haven't seen you in church in a while—where have you been?" "Well, Pastor, I've been going through some things." I have compassion for them, but I also think, *what is that all about?* They're allowing discomfort and hardships to influence and affect their commitment. They can't seem to separate how they feel from their actions, or their mood from their commitment. An emotional experience causes them to lose focus on the priorities in their life. They let how they *feel* influence what they *do.* Their feelings dictate how they react.

Jesus went about doing good regardless of the what, why, where, when, and how. Jesus never let a person, place, or thing stop Him. That's what we need to do, in spite of what's going on around us or what others are saying or doing to us. We need to rise above the moment, see beyond the temporary, and live and act our best.

••

We need to rise above the moment,
see beyond the temporary,
and live and act our best.

••

Don't Stop Doing

Sourena Vasseghi is my daughter-in love's brother. Sourena was born with cerebral palsy, which affects his motor and speech function. As a result, Sourena's body reflexes cause him to shake all the time; his head and feet are constantly moving and his communication is very slurred when he speaks. Yet this young man, in spite of cerebral palsy, graduated from high school and graduated from USC with a degree in business. He has also written a book that is a bestseller. A few years ago he got married and now he and his wife have two sons, Andrew and Tyler.

I'll never know the physical or emotional pain that Sourena goes through every day, but here's what I can tell you—he doesn't let the pain stop him. He does good even though there is pain in his life. He does more even though he has less-than-perfect circumstances. He may be in a wheelchair, but the wheelchair is not in him. He may have cerebral palsy, but cerebral palsy doesn't have him.

Sourena has risen above how he feels and does what is needed and what he wants to do. I've never seen him *not* try to engage in a conversation with someone even though it's difficult for him to speak. I've never seen him at an event hiding or isolating himself from the crowd. He just rolls on up in his chair and initiates the conversation. He always tries to smile and laugh, and when asked, he is willing to speak anywhere, *On How to Overcome,* using his computer! He's my hero! So I ask you, what's your excuse?

Helen Keller was born deaf and blind, yet she became a great political humanitarian. She was the first person with a severe disability to earn a degree. Ludwig von Beethoven was deaf by the age of 27, but he went on to compose some of the greatest symphonies the world has ever heard. Jackie Robinson, the first black person to enter into the major leagues, continued to perform in spite of the fact that no owner, team, or player wanted him to be part of baseball. Imagine the pressure, the stress, the discrimination, and the pain. It wasn't physical, it was emotional—but he battled and continued to perform and make his way to the batter's box. He kept swinging the bat. How about you?

I'm reminded of one story where Jackie was at his lowest point—he had been booed and sneered at by the fans after making an error. His own fans were booing him on the field. He said in his autobiography that it was a low point in his life and he thought, *You know, the battle is too big to fight. I'm just going to give up.* Emotionally and mentally, he was going to give up. And in that moment, Pee Wee Reese, who played shortstop, went out to him, and put his arm around Jackie, right in the middle of the game. The game stopped, and he stared down the entire crowd until there was silence. Looking back, Jackie said, "That's the moment where I broke through." There will be times when you are feeling bad and times when you're feeling your worst, but that's not the time for you to stop doing—it's not the time for you to stop giving your best.

Oftentimes, we let the hardships excuse our bad behavior: *Well, I have a right to feel this way! If you'd been through what I've been through, you'd see why it's not my fault. I'm just doing what I have to do. I can't help it. I'd be better, if you were better to me. I wouldn't be the way I am, if things were better. You just don't know.*

Whatever level of abuse, pain, or difficulty you have experienced in your life—don't use that as an excuse to give up. We are often quick to let circumstances justify our bad attitudes and behaviors, and some have perfected the excuse game. We play the blame game like Adam did with Eve, when he spoke to God about her in the Book of Genesis, "*The woman you gave me. She made me do it.*" We play the victim role. *It's not my fault. I'm innocent. Woe is me.* We play emotional dodgeball and set up our own rules, which include avoiding responsibility. *Who me? Not me? It's your fault. Sniffle, cry, tears.* You can practically hear the harp music playing in the background like an episode of *The Days of Our Lives.* So much drama! I'm reminded of Elijah running in fear from Jezebel. I'm sure he was thinking, *I have a right to be depressed and discouraged and defeated and suicidal. I have a right to quit and give up! I have a right to be mad and to be angry. Nobody knows what I'm going through or how I feel! I'm the only one living right and doing right! I'm the only one who cares.* And God responds by saying, "No. You're not the only one. There are 7,000 others that have not yet bowed their knee," (1 Kings 19:18).

In the tragic story of Naomi, we learn that she lost her husband and two sons. She and one of her daughters-in-law, Ruth, returned to Jerusalem. The Bible says that all the women in the city came out, and began to celebrate Naomi's return. Naomi looked at them and said, "Call me not Naomi, call me Mara because I'm a bitter woman and I'm empty," (Ruth 1:20-21 paraphrase). Maybe she thought that she had experienced too much hurt, pain, disappointment, and loss for God to care, restore, help, or change her outcome. Bitterness had caused Naomi to lose sight of her hope in God. But the end of Naomi's story reveals God's faithfulness to her. She had a grandson! "Blessed be the Lord, who has not left you this day without a close relative. . . . Naomi took the child, laid it on her bosom and became nurse to it," (Ruth 4:14,16). Wow, God restored Naomi!

We can't allow difficulties and hardships in our lives to be an excuse for dramatic changes in our behavior. A few years ago I was battling cancer. This was a very hard season in my life, and it took every ounce of energy to keep my spirits up day after day. I remember that during this time my personality began to change. I stopped smiling, I stopped singing, and I stopped initiating conversations with people. I was starting to do a little more accepting rather than reject-ing, when it came to my outlook, perspective, and attitude toward my circumstances. How I was feeling began to shape my reaction and response. Then one day I heard the gentle voice of the Holy Spirit whisper deep down inside of me,

"Diego, you're allowing this situation to form a new persona of who you are by the way you talk, how you behave, and interact with other people. You are starting to justify these changes, and if you don't stop, these behavior patterns will become permanent."

Sometimes we can be in a battle, a storm, or a hardship for so long that we forget the person that we used to be, before it all happened. We start walking around without a smile, a song, or the desire to reach out to others. We draw the shades down in our lives; play the "woe is me" sad songs, and start sucking sour lemons. Take a moment right now and think about something that you haven't done in a long time. What part of you haven't you let out to play? What new behavior changes have now become permanent parking signs in your life? Ask yourself, *what was the childlike version of me like, before all this bad stuff happened?*

Sometimes we can be in a battle, a storm,
or a hardship for so long that we forget
the person that we used to be.

There is an old story from back in the day when there were gas station attendants. This guy drives up to get gas, and he asked the attendant to clean his windows. And so the attendant cleans his windows. And the man looks out and says, "You didn't do a good job, can you do it again?" So the attendant does it again. Again the man says, "I still see all the stains and all the dirt. Clean it again, please." At that moment his wife, looks at him, takes off his glasses and says, "Why don't you just clean these?"

You see, the problem isn't always the windshield; sometimes it's the lens on your glasses. Could it be that they're all blurry and scratched up? If they are, then this might be what has tainted and altered your vision, outlook, and perspective. Let's not allow how we feel affect how we see or do life. We can rise above emotions, moods, and feelings and give our best, even if we don't feel our best. Jesus knows how we feel because He experienced it all, and will help us to react like He did! What a blessing and witness we would be in our homes, marriages, families, jobs, and relationships, if we were not governed by our feelings. Today violence, abuse, feuding, and fighting is caused by people who let how they feel determine what they do and how they react. They let bad moments turn into bad lives. They let disappointments and rejections control their decisions. They stop doing what they were doing before the unpleasant circumstance, and start going in the opposite direction.

I remember when I was a teenager, I had a 1965 Volkswagen. It was the first car I bought. I worked hard and saved $1,200.00 to buy it. It took me the whole summer of 1978 (sounds like a song), and I named my car Herbie. Herbie and I were cool cruising buddies. Well, the car was stolen from my parents' front yard. My heart was broken. The police called and said it was in a salvage yard and to come and get it. I was so happy over the news. I went with my mom to get it. It was like a reunion from a movie as I ran slowly toward my Volkswagen with the sun shining on him. He glistened in the sun. It was perfect until we walked to the other side of the car and low and behold, it was totaled like a crushed can.

"*Noooooo!*" I cried. I told my mom with sorrow and grief, "I don't want it any more. Let the salvage yard have it. I'm going to abandon old Herbie and reminisce and dream about the memories we once had!" My mom said, 'No, we are towing him home and you are going to earn money and put your Volkswagen back on the road." Long story short, we did and he did. Beep, beep, beep! Herbie and I were on the road again!

Seven Pictures of Jesus

If there was ever anyone that could justify choosing selfishness versus selflessness, it would have been Jesus. And that's really what it boils down to in those moments when we are not doing good because we feel bad—selfishness versus selflessness. Have you ever told someone, "*don't bother me. Don't call me. Don't text me. Don't disturb me. I'm not feeling good today. Just leave me alone! I'm having a really bad day!*" Maybe you've never actually told someone this, but all of us have at least thought it. I'm going to give you seven examples from Jesus' life when things were definitely not going good. But in each of these situations, Jesus never said, "*don't bother me!*" Or, "*I have a right and a reason to be less than good!*"

CHAPTER 1

....

"The man who lives by himself and for himself is
likely to be corrupted by the company he keeps."
—Charles H. Parkhurst

....

The first example is found in the book of Matthew. "So
[Herod] sent and had John beheaded in prison. And his head
was brought on a platter and given to a girl, and she brought
it to her mother. Then his disciples came and took away the
body and buried it, and went and told Jesus," (Matthew
14:10-12) What did the disciples tell Jesus? That his cousin,
John the Baptist, had been killed and beheaded!
Understandably, Jesus wanted to be alone. "He departed from
there by boat to a deserted place by Himself. But when the
multitudes heard it, they followed Him on foot from the cities.
And when Jesus went out He saw a great multitude; and He
was moved with compassion for them, and healed their sick,"
(Matthew 14:13-14).

Have you ever lost a loved one? It's pretty tough. It's
painful. It's one of the emptiest feelings that anyone can experience. And Jesus went through it, too. John the Baptist was
His cousin and there was a very close connection between
them. I think it was because John the Baptist was the only
person that recognized who Jesus truly was. He was the first
person outside of God to declare, "This is God's son, the
Lamb of God who takes away the sins of the world. Behold,
the Lamb of God!" John knew His calling. He knew His
purpose. He was the one that went before Jesus and prepared
the way. He baptized Jesus in the River Jordan and two of

Jesus' Apostles, Andrew and Peter, were the first followers of John. John said the memorable words, "He must increase but I must decrease" and "whose sandal strap I am not worthy to lose." There was definitely a close binding intimate connection between the two of them. (See John 1:27; John 3:30). In the scriptures, Jesus shows us a great picture of what to do when we experience loss. *He withdrew to a solitary place;* He went to be alone with the Father. Jesus was feeling all the grief and emotions that one can feel, in the midst of His pain, sorrow, and sadness. He first went to be alone with His Father, knowing that He was the only one who could help. He didn't seek comfort from Jack Daniels and Jim Bean. He didn't get alone with drugs or the internet. He didn't drown His sorrows in a gallon of ice cream or a box of chocolates.

If there was ever a time for Jesus to be selfish and say, "Don't bother me! Can't you see I'm grieving, and I'm hurting right now? I don't want to go to church! I don't want to pray right now! I don't want to sing those songs right now! I don't want to be a husband or wife or father or mother. I want to be sad. I quit! I can't take it anymore, and I'm just going to stop," this was it. But Jesus didn't do that. Jesus chose to do good when He was feeling bad.

There is absolutely nothing wrong with the emotions of sadness or sorrow. Jesus is our example of how we should process the questions of "how, what, and why," in the midst of our loss. Jesus didn't let how He felt dictate how He would act, or what He would do! In spite of what He felt, He gave His best. Jesus did the opposite of what the enemy wanted or what He felt like doing. Instead, He had compassion on the sick and healed them. He gave, He helped, and He served others. He didn't stop being Jesus!

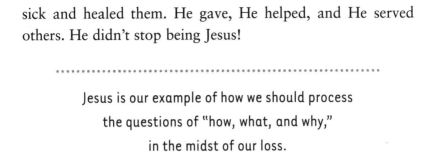

Jesus is our example of how we should process the questions of "how, what, and why," in the midst of our loss.

The second example of Jesus doing good is found in the book of John. It says, "When Jesus had said these things, He was troubled in spirit, and testified and said, 'Most assuredly, I say to you, one of you will betray Me,'" (John 13:21). Now, Jesus had just finished washing all twelve of the disciples' feet and they were all partaking of Holy Communion—including Judas. They had just finished a lovely dinner at a five star restaurant with a seven course meal and laughter and conversation. I'm exaggerating a little, but Judas was still among them. Jesus knew that Judas was going to betray Him. I find it quite interesting that Jesus didn't discriminate or show partiality at that vulnerable time. He could have easily turned away from Judas, showing displeasure, meanness, or hatred. He could have displayed a vengeful attitude and disgust towards Judas, but He didn't.

Think about it for a minute. If you knew someone was talking about you, lying, stealing, and getting ready to betray you, wouldn't you show some sign of anger or dissatisfaction? You might look at them a little weird or give them the evil eye or at least slap them, then apologize later. I'm just kidding. If you were in Jesus' shoes, you might say something like, "You know what, I can't say which one of you is a betrayer and a back stabber! A no good blankity-blank, but one of you here, who is seated three seats away from me, and you're wearing a blue coat, and brown sandals, and you've got brown eyes, and you're about 5'8. And your initials are J.I. and you're in charge of the money bag. But I can't say who you are."

Betrayal is no picnic, and it's important to recognize Jesus wasn't feeling very good right then, concerning the whole situation that was about to go down. I'm sure there were feelings of sadness, heartache, and brokenness, but how He handled the moment is an amazing epic story. How do you handle betrayal? How do you handle people that offend you? Do you look weird at them? Do you stare them down? Do you give them the cold shoulder? Do you ignore them? I would probably slip and say something to them. But Jesus didn't.

Jesus does good by washing Judas' feet, and serving him communion. He gives him bread and wine without spitting in it or spilling it on him. Maybe even poisoning it. Jesus gives His best when feeling His worst. He does the opposite of what someone expects or desires. Doing good to someone not because they do good, but because God has been good to you. This is what he is displaying here. Jesus gives the same love and service to Judas as the other eleven disciples. Doing good for someone because we are supposed to do good.

A third example of Jesus doing good even when He was feeling bad is found in Luke. "And while He was still speaking, behold, a multitude; and he who was called Judas, one of the twelve, went before them and drew near to Jesus to kiss Him," (Luke 22:47). This story takes place in the Garden of

Gethsemane. The book of Matthew adds more detail as to how Jesus was feeling at that moment, saying this, "Then He said to them, My soul is exceedingly sorrowful, even to death. Stay here and watch with Me," (Matthew 26:38). Yes, the cross of Calvary was an intensely excruciating time for Jesus, but the Garden of Gethsemane was a really, really tough time too.

Jesus was under such stress, anguish, and exhaustion that the Bible says, "He was sweating, oozing and dripping blood out of His forehead," (Luke 22:44). The pain was so great it felt like He would die. What was happening to cause so much anguish? Could it be Jesus was seeing Himself separated from the Father? Was He seeing the Cross becoming a reality in His life? The judgement of God was in full motion. Jesus knew all the sins of mankind would be put upon Him. Could it be He was experiencing emotions of the unknown? The struggle of obeying God and possibly much more?

He then asked His disciples, *"would you pray with Me,"* but they couldn't even pray for one hour. Jesus didn't ask for much personally, but the one time He asked for help from His followers, they didn't come through. I wonder how long they actually prayed or attempted to pray. Suddenly, all the soldiers show up with lanterns, clubs, and swords. The Sanhedrin religious leaders surrounded Him. Then His friend, who He spent more than three years with, comes and *kisses Him* on the cheek to point Him out and says, *"He's the one."* Judas' betrayal was complete. Wow, he kissed Jesus. The kiss of betrayal that says, "I don't need you anymore," a kiss to say goodbye. I think every pastor of a church has had that kiss. So long, *adios, sayonara*, have a nice day.

What happens next is so interesting. Peter, like a samurai or a homeboy from the streets or maybe a butcher at a deli, takes his sword and chops off the ear of a guard named Malchus. Then Jesus, in the midst of His sorrow, stops and picks the ear up off the ground, touches, heals, and restores Malchus' ear. In the middle of the chaos and screaming, a crisis moment, *Jesus is totally in control.* How does Jesus handle this moment of stress, pressure, anguish, and disappointment? Does He cuss everyone out? Does He pick up a stick and start hitting Peter, James, and John, because they promised to pray and didn't come through? Does He give in to the circumstance, to justify an action? Does He become selfish and self-centered and say to Malchus, who is screaming at the top of his voice, *"You shouldn't have messed with me! Sorry no more healing or miracles available!"* Does Jesus look at Peter and say, *"You're going to jail and die, because you put your hand on a Roman soldier. Too bad, so sad! I can't help you right now! I have my own problems."* Does Jesus cuss at Judas like a sailor and tell him he's going to hell? No! He continues doing good when He's feeling bad. He gives His best when feeling His worst. He continues to serve, heal, and put the needs and concerns of others above Himself.

How do you feel or react when someone gives you the goodbye kiss of rejection? How do you feel or react when someone is experiencing pain, and are getting what they deserve? Is there any sympathy or empathy on your part or do you say to yourself, *he deserves it.* Ouch!

A fourth example of Jesus doing good when He's feeling bad is the story of the enemy tempting Him in the wilderness.

CHAPTER 1

The Bible says, "Then Jesus was led up by the Spirit into the wilderness to be tempted by the devil. And when He had fasted forty days and forty nights, afterward He was hungry," (Matthew 4:1-2).

Jesus was in the midst of three separate temptations in the wilderness. We don't know how long He was tempted, whether it was the full length of the 40 days, but we do know that they were great temptations. The Bible tells us that after the temptations, angels came to minister to Him. Just ponder that for a moment. How do you think they ministered to Him? What did they do? We don't know. We can only speculate. Did they feed Him a meal? Did they bring Him some water? Did they sit down next to Him and put their arms around Him? Did they sing Him a song or quote scripture to Him? Did they say, *"You did a great job? You won! You are a winner! We love you!"*

I don't know exactly what they did, but the Bible says Jesus was exhausted. But notice what He does while being tempted. He keeps quoting the Word over and over. Jesus answered, "It is written . . . It is written . . . It is written," (Matthew 4:4-11). He just kept quoting the Word, repeating the scripture, and speaking the Bible promises!

When we are having a bad moment in our life, when we are not feeling our best, or when unfortunate circumstances are happening, what should we do? We are to keep speaking the Word, "It is written." Keep speaking the promises of God over your life and over the life of others. What we speak during times of weariness, exhaustion, and temptation, are essential to us winning in life. There's nothing negative or fearful coming out of Jesus' mouth!'

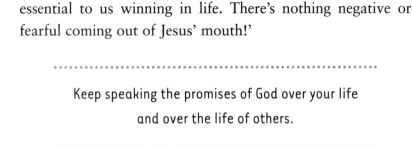

Keep speaking the promises of God over your life and over the life of others.

One of my heroes is John Harper. He was a pastor in Glasgow, Scotland. He was given a church of 25 people and it grew to 500. John Harper was one of the passengers on the Titanic when it sank. He was there with his daughter and his sister. When the disaster hit, the women were the first to board the rafts. John's daughter and sister were rescued. While John Harper waited to board a raft, he did something amazing. He plunged into the 30 degree Atlantic Ocean, amidst the chaos, the screaming, and the confusion of that moment. This was a bad situation, not to mention the frigid water!

If that happened to me, I don't know what I would do. I'd be looking for something or someone to hold onto. In times of desperation, people will do just about anything to stay afloat. Every man for himself, right?! Not John Harper. Instead, he swam toward every single person he could reach within the last few moments of his life and declared, "Believe on the Lord Jesus Christ and you will be saved," (Acts 16:31). He would ask, *"Are you saved? Do you know Jesus as your Lord? Don't perish! Accept Him and repent."* And then he died.

When feeling bad, we must keep doing good, like Jesus, and keep speaking the Word of God over our situation, and to others. Don't speak what you feel. Don't speak failure and defeat. Don't speak the problem. Talk back to the devil when he tries to hold conversations with you, and he will leave; you must do as Jesus did, repeat the word of God. "Then the devil left him and behold angels came and ministered to Him," (Matthew 4:11).

The fifth example, of Jesus doing good when feeling bad, is at the Cross. Jesus was thinking about the care of his mother, Mary. He said to John, the disciple, "Behold your mother," and at the end of this verse it says, "the disciple took her to live with him," (See John 19:27). To the thief hanging on the cross next to him, Jesus said, "Today you will be with me in paradise." To those killing him, Jesus said; "Forgive them for they know not what they do." These three powerful episodes at the cross were a total display of Jesus' unselfish, sacrificial love for mankind. Even at the time of his own death, he continued to care for others.

Jesus was on the cross, enduring the greatest pain in the entire universe. Not just the physical suffering of the crucifixion, but even greater. He was suffering the wrath and judgment of God, and separation from the Father. Every sin of all mankind—past, present, and future—was being poured out upon Him. In that moment, He could have said, *"Don't bother me! I have a right to be really selfish right now. I'm on a cross— what do you want? Not now, you've got to be kidding."* No, Jesus didn't do that. Instead, while He was in the worst pain of His life, He was thinking about the care, protection, and provision of His mother, Mary. He was thinking about a thief on a cross. He was thinking about people who didn't understand what they were doing.

Mary Johnson understood that kind of pain. A man named Oshea Israel killed her 20-year-old son in 1993. Mary Johnson chose to do good in the midst of feeling bad. She went to visit the man in prison who murdered her son. As she stood face to face with him she chose to forgive him. The man was overwhelmed by the love this mother showed him. Since his release from prison Oshea and Mary have remained friends and are now neighbors. She watches after him and he watches after her. A former murderer who killed a mother's son has become a best friend and part of the family. How does that happen? It's only possible with Jesus.

Jesus, in the midst of His pain, was thinking about the pain of others; *His grieving mother, her losses, her loneliness, and her security; the thief, his salvation and his everlasting eternal life; and those who condemned Him, they needed His forgiveness.* He was putting their needs, concerns, and issues before His own. Jesus made Himself available. He could have had a "do not disturb" sign hanging on His neck, but instead He allowed Himself to be interrupted and inconvenienced. When we look at the beginning of His ministry, we learn that *He went about doing good and healing all who were oppressed by the devil.* Jesus always did good from beginning to end, He was always giving. This wasn't something He did once in a while or during the good days when He was popular. No, He did it to the very end, when He uttered his famous last words, *It is finished.* What does that say to you?

Have you ever heard the saying, "Where there is no pain, there is no gain?" There are all kinds of pain in our lives— there is no way around it. But we can use our pain to make lifelong changes. We can use our pain to help others and make a difference. God doesn't waste our pain. If we let Him, He will use it. It's hard for us to conceive that from great pain, a new purpose can begin to emerge, especially if you are in the midst of the pain.

God doesn't waste our pain.
If we let Him, He will use it.

You may be in pain right now, but I want to challenge you to be like Jesus and do good when you're feeling bad; to give your best when you're feeling your worst. God doesn't ever waste pain. Let it propel you to do great things in the kingdom of God. Allow your pain to drive you toward a place in God you've never been before.

The sixth example of Jesus doing good when feeling bad, is the pressure people tried to put on Him to be a revolutionist. They wanted Him to take over the Roman Empire; to raise up an army of followers, who would revolt against Rome, build a kingdom on this earth, and make Himself a King with a throne (John 6:15). But He didn't let the pressure force Him to become something other than what He had been called to do.

The devil will pressure us to sin, lie, cheat, and steal. He will use friends to pressure us to go to places we should avoid, and do things we shouldn't do. Sometimes, pressure can get us into following the latest fads and even political correctness trends, just so we won't offend anyone. Christians are under pressure to stop believing in the Bible, marriage, hell, judgment, and in the sanctity of life.

Parents, sometimes, pressure their children to follow the career choice that they choose for them. Spouses can put pressure on their mate to make a certain amount of money so they can live a certain lifestyle. The pressures can cause us to work and stay at a job that is uncomfortable, questionable or maybe even unethical, for fear of losing the job and the money. These are real pressures we face from strangers, friends, and loved ones. But we must follow the way of Jesus by not letting society influence us to be something that God has not created us to be. We too must repeat the words that Jesus said, *"for I always do those things that please Him,"* (John 8:29). Pressure can make you stop doing good and giving your best.

The seventh example Jesus dealt with while doing good, was the rumors and accusations surrounding His birth. The continuous gossiping and finger pointing behind his back, with statements like: *"Could He be someone else's baby? Who is the real father? Who was Mary really with? What is the true story of her pregnancy?"* There will always be skeptics who will try to change the narrative and question the legitimacy of the virgin birth. Jesus had to face mocking and continual harassment with rumors, speculations, and accusations.

Harassment is a part of our society today with kids who don't think twice about intimidating and mocking fellow students. They think it's ok to tease and call their peers names. Day after day, children are faced with bullies who make fun of them, especially if a kid is different and hasn't learned how to deal with bulling. They are called "pee wee" because they're small, "four eyes" because they wear glasses, "pizza face" because they have acne, or "giraffe" because they are tall. These children live in fear because of the constant harassment from bullies who are rarely confronted, which seems to legitimize their negative behavior.

Jesus continued doing good and giving His best in the face of harassments and accusations. He didn't stop, He didn't change course or defect from His calling. He didn't allow the relentless whispers, rolling eyes, and rumors of his legitimacy stop him. Wow! In those days, towns were much smaller so everyone knew your business. "Then they said to Him, 'Where is Your Father?' Jesus answered, 'You know neither Me nor My Father. If you had known Me, you would have known My Father also. You do the deeds of your father.' Then they said to Him, 'We were not born of fornication; we have one Father—God,'" (John 8:19,41). Notice the word "Father" and "born of fornication." Jesus was being labeled and branded. Jesus was being gossiped about and discredited all the time. They were always trying to deny His legitimacy by saying He was illegitimate.

Imagine how real that attack was. It's amazing how people will conveniently change the truth to fit their narrative. The Pharisees were well versed in the prophesy of the coming Messiah, but they had amnesia when it came to Jesus. "Therefore the Lord Himself will give you a sign: Behold, the virgin shall conceive and bear a Son, and shall call His name Immanuel," (Isaiah 7:14).

Even though Jesus went about doing good throughout his ministry, the skeptics and doubters still labeled Him. The ongoing gossiping at the local market and coffee shop. Imagine what lies and false stories the news media of the day were reporting. Yet, in spite of all these words and expressions of hostility and hatred and ill–feelings towards Jesus, He still continued to love, forgive, and serve. He never quit or gave up on His calling, assignment, mission, and purpose. He never stopped being Christ. Likewise we should never stop being a Christian. He never let people's actions influence His reaction, attitude or response. He kept giving His best when He felt His worst! He never lowered Himself to the people's standards. He never got into a fight or yelling match, trying to defend His honor. Jesus never let the environment affect His temperature.

CHAPTER 2

*For He shall grow up before Him as a tender plant,
and as a root out of dry ground; He has no form or
comeliness; and when we see Him, there is no beauty
that we should desire Him.*

—Isaiah 53:2

These days people want drama-free lives—no hassle, no
waiting, no discomfort, and no interruptions—but the truth is
that we are all going to experience pain, discomfort, and hardship in this world. Jesus said, "I have told you these things, so
that in Me you may have [perfect] peace. In the world you
have tribulation and distress and suffering, but be courageous
[be confident, be undaunted, be filled with joy]; I have overcome the world [My conquest is accomplished, My victory
abiding]," (John 16:33 AMP). Unfortunately, when those
trials and tribulations come, not all of us are going to keep
doing good, keep giving our best, and keep moving forward.
Many will slow down, hesitate, or just give up. Our actions
and our attitudes will resonate loudly when we say, *I'm done
with* this, or it's all over.

Anyone can perform well when the wind is at our back and the sun is shining brightly—when the marriage, kids, money, joy, and health are good. However, when our lives aren't perfect it often becomes an excuse to fall short. Some might say, "*I need to have a perfect marriage before I can walk in love. I need my finances to be just right with plenty left over before I can give into God's Kingdom. I need less busyness in my life before I can attend church, volunteer, or help.*"

I'm reminded of the story in 2 Kings 4:8-37 about the Shulamite woman whose son died. What's important about this story is how she reacted when hearing the news about her son. When questioned about his death, she repeatedly responded, "*It is well, It is well.*" God honored her faith and used the prophet to heal her son. This is a great example of what we're talking about.

The sad truth is most people live their lives according to how they feel. If they don't *feel* like praying, or they don't *feel* like reading the Bible, or they don't *feel* like fasting, or they don't *feel* like worshiping, or they don't *feel* like tithing, or walking in forgiveness, eventually, they won't *feel* like going to church. These are all the spiritual disciplines that draw us closer to Jesus. If we begin to live by our feelings alone it can lead us to a multitude of problems that will affect our emotional life. Sometimes we have to rise above the environment that is around us and still perform. We live in a sin-filled world, and if we're waiting for things to be "perfect," we're never going to "do good" as a Christian with that kind of mentality.

David Livingston, the famous missionary, said, "I'll do anything as long as it's forward." We have to learn how to go forward even when we are going against a strong head wind. We need to do good when we are surrounded by people that are hard to like on the job; when we have bad neighbors; when we have a terrible marriage or wayward children. We have to learn how to do good when our body isn't feeling well, or when we've lost our job. Doing our best and giving our best when we feel like we are at our worst, is what it's all about! *Farmers who wait for perfect weather never plant. If they watch every cloud, they never harvest.*

There is a reason why the Bible calls us *overcoming Christians* (1 John 4:4 AMP), *conquering Christians* (Romans 8:37 AMP), *victorious Christians* (1 Corinthians 15:57 AMP), and *empowering Christians* (Philippians 4:13 AMP). These are not bumper stickers or T-shirt slogans. They are not just magical mantras that we repeat over and over to pump ourselves up. No, we are overcomers because He overcame. We are conquerors because He defeated death and rose from the grave. We are victorious because He gave us our Lord Jesus Christ. We are triumphant because He gives us strength.

We are overcomers because He overcame.

How are we able to overcome? When we receive Christ the Holy Spirit and His anointing power comes and abides in us. In 1 John 2:27 it says, "But the anointing that you received from Him abides in you." The church uses that word, *anointed*, all the time, but many of us don't actually know what it means. *That was an anointed service. That was an*

anointed message. Man, the anointing of God was upon you!
For those who are new to Christianity or a unchurched
person, this word is used quite often—"How God anointed
Jesus of Nazareth with the Holy Spirit and with power, who
went about doing good and healing all who were oppressed
by the devil, for God was with Him," (Acts 10:38). I like to
look at it this way—the anointing of God represents the favor
of God, as well as His power and His tangible or manifested
presence. So when we say, "That was anointed," we're really
saying, "It was favored by God." We're also saying that there
is a physical manifestation of God's presence or power that is
tangible and distinguishably moving in our midst.

Do you ever say, "God has anointed me"? Well, you
should! A good question to ask yourself would be, "*Why* has
He anointed me?" Do you think it's so that you can go about
and do nothing? No! To be nothing. No! To have nothing.
No! Maybe it's so that you can go about and *do good*. When
God's anointing is with you, you are able to take God's favor
and tangible presence wherever you go and make a difference. Even in the midst of the most dire situation, that's what
the anointing is for. The anointing of God upon you, is to
help you perform, accomplish and fulfill your mission to do
good. The anointing of God is not for you to look holy, spiritual, to fall down, shout, and run around in the church. God
has anointed you to perform in unattractive places with unattractive people. No matter what, don't let that stop you! You
are anointed to be a great spouse, parent, employee,
employer, student, or friend. Remember, whatever your voca-
tion or occupation is, the favor of God goes with you so you
can do good.

CHAPTER 2

Grow in Dry Ground

It's amazing how we can overcome obstacles if we have a goal that we think is pleasurable or appealing. For instance, we might not really mind putting our body through sleep deprivation, if we get to stay out late with someone we really like. We stress out our body working overtime to accomplish our goals. We save to go on a great vacation; buy something we really want; or will even lose weight to go to the high school reunion.

When we compare this to obstacles that resemble hardship or difficulty related to our faith, spirituality, or obedience to God, we often have zero tolerance, motivation, endurance, effort, or commitment. We become sluggish, lazy, and slothful. In fact, when we go through difficulties, most of us would mimic the lyrics of an old Beatles' song:

Don't Bother Me.
So go away and leave me alone,
I've got no time for you right now.
Don't come around, leave me alone,
Don't bother me.

Have you ever said that to someone? *"Don't bother me; I'm eating! Don't bother me; I'm tired! Don't mess with me today! This just isn't a good day! Why are you always bothering me!"* Not Jesus. Nowhere in the scriptures do we see Him ever saying anything like that. Jesus was surrounded by hardship, yet He went about *doing good*, no matter the state of His *feelings, surroundings, and environment.* He grew and thrived in foreign dry ground.

Growing in dry ground—a place with no life-giving water—seems to go against the natural order of things. If a farmer plants a crop and doesn't water it, without fail it will die. And yet that's exactly what God wants us to be able to do—to not just *survive,* but *thrive* when we are out of our element, just like Jesus did. He was able to grow even in famine situations, in wilderness conditions, and in the desolate places. When no one believed in Him; when He had little support and little encouragement, He grew, He increased, He multiplied, and He advanced. Are you getting the picture?

> Jesus was surrounded by hardship,
> yet He went about *doing good,*
> no matter the state of His feelings,
> surroundings, and environment.

We think we need the perfect situation or environment to give our best, thrive, or perform well, but the Bible doesn't promise perfection. Instead, it tells us that we should be able to grow where we aren't supposed to grow. Grow when there's little to no support. Grow when you feel dry, bored, and tired. The Bible is full of examples of God's people thriving in places that were dry ground. Daniel, Shadrach, Meshach, and Abednego, Joseph, Nehemiah, and even Esther—all found themselves in a foreign environment that was far from perfect. They often had little support and little to write home about! In fact, their environments were often hostile and filled with persecution.

Perhaps you know someone personally who has been able to grow in dry ground. Countless people with physical or mental disabilities are able to grow and thrive every day, overcoming all kinds of natural limitations and challenges. There are people who have been incarcerated in prison and yet find a way to make something of prison life; some of whom go on to do great things when they are released. People who have health issues start programs to help those who are sick. People who struggled or experienced something devastating in their life, use their experience to go back and help those still struggling with the same issues they once had. Nelson Mandela was one of those individuals. He became educated in prison and used that education to his advantage, eventually going on to become the president of South Africa. He was in prison but prison wasn't in him. He knew he was coming out! Twenty-seven years of confinement, darkness, loneliness, and persecution. Like Joseph in the Bible, from a prison cell to the palace.

Some people have lost everything, yet still have found a way to succeed and rebuild their lives. Henry Ford failed five times. R.H. Macy failed seven times. Soichiro Honda was not hired by Toyota. Harland David Sanders failed 109 times before he mastered his world-famous secret chicken recipe. Walt Disney was fired by a newspaper and 300 banks turned him down for a loan for Disneyland, and Charles Shultz the creator of the famous *Peanuts* character was not hired by Walt Disney. Cha Sa-soon failed 950 times trying to get her driver's license, but at 69 years old this grandmother finally got it.

All of these people grew, even though at some point in their lives they all walked through dry ground. They overcame the odds, rejections, denials, bad conditions and circumstances. The people in these stories were real and they lived to tell the world of their experiences, and the perseverance it took to be their best. You too, can grow, be fruitful and bountiful and give your best in dry ground. It doesn't matter how broken, shattered, damaged, or disadvantaged your childhood, teenage, or adult years have been; God grows and causes you to bud, sprout, and bear fruit when others say, *"it's impossible, it's never going to happen, or it's too far gone!"* That's what was said about me in 2008, when I had terminal cancer stage 4 and given a 50 percent chance to live one year. But God! Don't let the dry ground in your life make you dry!

Doing Good With Detours or Distractions

Jesus was on a mission. He had a job to do for His Father, and there was no time to waste. He didn't just wake up one day, stretch, yawn, and say to Himself, "I'm just going to wander through Judea and just see what happens. I'll just fly by the seat of my pants and what will be, will be!"

No, Jesus had a mission-driven life. Jesus had places to go and people to see. He had a schedule to keep just like you and I, but He was constantly interrupted and disturbed by the detours. And yet in spite of all the diversions, distractions, and inconveniences, He kept doing good and giving His best. We read about one of those moments in the book of Mark,

"Immediately many gathered together, so that there was no longer room to receive them, not even near the door. And He preached the word to them. Then they came to Him, bringing a paralytic who was carried by four men. And when they could not come near Him because of the crowd, they uncovered the roof where He was. So when they had broken through, they let down the bed on which the paralytic was lying," (Mark 2:2-4).

For just a moment, imagine yourself being there in this scenario. Jesus was preaching the Word to a packed room with standing room only. He was preaching a great message and was probably coming to the climax—the very thing He wanted everyone to hear. Maybe there were some Amen's, Hallelujah's, and preach it statements being heard (not really); when suddenly a little dust starts dropping from the ceiling. Nobody notices at first. But then twigs start dropping on the ground. Then clumps of clay fall. All of a sudden you look up and sunlight is streaming through the roof. By now, nobody is listening to Jesus. Everyone is focused on the voices above, followed by a rope, a pallet, and strong hands lowering a grown man down through the roof to the feet of Jesus. Talk about an unexpected turn of events! *How rude is that!? Don't they know protocol? Wow, why are they interrupting? Did they have an appointment? Did they call Jesus' personal assistant first?* But Jesus responds with a great attitude by healing the paralytic man.

A second example is found in the book of Luke, when Jesus is on His way to heal Jairus' sick daughter and a woman with an issue of blood (blood disease), interrupts Him.

Basically, she cuts in line and her actions are saying, *me first*, while she's pulling on Jesus' coat. How did Jesus respond? The scripture reads, "And He said to her, 'Daughter, be of good cheer; your faith has made you well. Go in peace,'" (Mark 5:21-43).

Another time, Jesus was at a wedding, simply enjoying being a guest with His mother and disciples. When the wine was gone, Jesus' mother said to him, "they have no more wine." Now Jesus might have been telling a story, dancing, laughing, or just relaxing. He could have said, "don't bother me, I don't want to perform miracles today," but to save the day, He allowed himself to be interrupted, honored his mother's request and performed His first miracle by turning water into wine (John 2:1-11).

One day Jesus was walking down the road, minding His own business, when He was interrupted by a blind man named Bartimaeus, who yelled out several times at the top of his voice, *"Jesus, Son of David, have mercy upon me!"* (Mark 10:46-52). How did Jesus respond? Did he say, "be quiet, you are too loud, stop yelling at me, you're bothering me, I can't hear myself. . . ." No, Jesus stopped and said "your faith has healed you."

If you read through the New Testament, you will recognize the number of times Jesus' attention was diverted and interrupted by people like Bartimaeus. Jesus always met the challenge by keeping his composure. He stayed focused, blessed people, and touched lives by performing miracles.

The overall story of Jesus is that He did good under pressure. Jesus gave His best when He could have been full of excuses and reasons why He couldn't help people. He was willing to be interrupted and detained. He was willing to take the detour of opportunity. He made himself available. Some of His greatest miracles occurred because He allowed himself to be disturbed and inconvenienced. Jesus didn't look at interruption as a frustrating obstacle, but welcomed the chance to touch hurting people.

So let me ask you this question: *Can someone bother you? Or do you say to yourself, Don't bother me on Monday, because that's my family day. And don't bother me on Tuesday; because that's the time I watch my favorite show. Don't bother me on Wednesday, because I have church, and on Thursday I work out, and on Friday, I . . .*

....

Jesus didn't look at interruption
as a frustrating obstacle, but welcomed
the chance to touch hurting people.

....

When can God interrupt us? When can God take us on a detour? Is there ever a perfect time to witness to somebody? Is there ever a wrong time for someone to come up and say, *"Can you pray for me?"* Is there ever an easy time in our busy schedules to stop for someone who is a new convert in the kingdom of God and begin to disciple them and help to grow them in their faith? Can God interrupt our lunch hour? *God, are you serious! You know I'm hungry and I only get thirty minutes for lunch!* Can God interrupt our vacation? *Oh God, I worked hard all year and I'm on vacation!* Or how about interrupting you while you are sleeping, or at Starbucks getting a Grande latte with whipped cream? Maybe on an airplane flight where you just want to read, work, or sleep, and the person next to you wants to talk. Oh my! What should our words and attitude be like when these things happen?

Jesus teaches us how to serve through His example. When your best-laid plans have been interrupted, can you still serve? When your precious time has been interrupted, can you still give it joyfully? When you are feeling uncomfortable because of the demand that someone has placed on you, can you be obedient to the voice of the Holy Spirit, when He asks you to change your plans? When you've already given and given, and your tank is on empty, can you still answer the call for help? It's in those moments when the Holy Spirit wants to remind you about the goodness of Jesus, and how much He loves *you*. And you say to yourself, *okay that's enough! Knock it off! It's time for you to* be *your best even though you feel your worst.*

It happened to me recently with a family disagreement and ministry problem that got me upset and I felt like an angry dog, growling and barking at everyone that looked in my direction. I'm ashamed to say that it lasted a whole day. Then the thought came to me, *this doesn't feel right. This attitude doesn't fit who I am, nor does it reflect how good God has been to me.* So I stopped, changed my attitude to line up with Jesus, and started giving and being my best!

Everyone who crossed Jesus' path was touched and changed forever. The woman at the well had a spiritual cleansing when Jesus offered her living water of grace by forgiving her sins. And Simon of Cyrene, who carried Jesus' cross—at first glance, it may seem insignificant, but it meant a great deal to the One that he was made to help. This one event marked the date that Simon was given the opportunity to fulfill his purpose. He had a life-changing encounter with Jesus. God considered this act important enough to mention it three times in His word (Matthew 27:32, Mark 15:21, Luke 23:26).

When Criticism Comes

Jesus teaches us another truth through his example. We have to learn to do good even when we are being criticized. "And while He was being accused by the chief priests and elders, He answered nothing," (Matthew 27:12). Sometimes that's the only way to handle criticism. When Jesus was being criticized by the high priest, what did He do? Did He defend Himself? Start having a debate? Try to validate His ministry? No, what does He do? *He says nothing.*

Throughout the scriptures, we see that these religious leaders were always watching Jesus, taking notes to see if He was going to do something wrong. "So the scribes and Pharisees watched Him closely, whether He would heal on the Sabbath, that they might find an accusation against Him," (Luke 6:7). These weren't favorable eyes watching Him. These were eyes that wanted to find something they could use to defeat Him. These leaders were always staring Him down, following Him from a distance and spying. They were always interviewing people that had encounters with Jesus, trying to find something they could use to discredit Him. They were there, watching His every move, always lurking in the shadows, like raging hyenas or vultures encircling and waiting for the kill.

Imagine that tension. Imagine that stress following you everywhere you go. You go to the market, people are there watching everything you do. You go to the mall, people are there with binoculars. *"I think He's pulling out a $100 bill. Yep! Oh my . . . he's buying some Versace sandals right now, for $733!"* Always looking! Even going through your trash cans. Judging you for eating lobster, which costs $26.99 a pound, because after all, *there are hungry and homeless people in this city!*

This was almost an everyday ritual for Jesus in His ministry—everywhere He walked, when He talked, what He ate, where He slept—and make no mistake, they did it to His disciples, too. You talk about pressure! You talk about stress! But He kept giving His best. He kept preaching, teaching, and healing. He never let their criticism stop Him.

So what does this mean to us? It means we have to learn how to handle the criticism and how to be longsuffering, forgiving, and learn to let things go. Believe me, if you aren't being criticized, you aren't doing anything of significance. If everyone likes you and says pleasant things about you, then you aren't doing much to make the devil upset. If you want to live your life doing good like Jesus, you will *always* be criticized for what you do. Here are some thoughts about criticism:

- Whatever you do that's good or bad, people will always have something negative to say.

- People that criticize your life usually don't know the price you paid to get where you are today.
- Don't let compliments get to your head, and don't let their criticism get to your heart.
- You will never be able to please an unhappy person.
- Ten to twenty percent of all groups are critics.

I remember a time, when a member of our church was having marital problems. The couple would sit on the front row, Sunday after Sunday, listening to the sermons. Within a short while I began to hear that the husband had started spreading rumors about me. This baffled me, because I would see him and his wife every Sunday. Well, after careful investigation, I found out that his wife would go home and say to her husband, "Why can't you be nice like Pastor Diego is to his wife, Cindy?" and she would follow it up by playing the comparison game between her husband and me. Oh my, not recommended! Needless to say the man started inventing lies about me. He started attacking my name by making false statements about my character. This incident put me in a bad position. I felt like I had to defend myself for something I hadn't said or done to either the man or the woman. It made me feel uneasy, but every Sunday, I had to preach with that man sitting right in front of me, judging me and criticizing me based on his false perception. But I had to smile. *I wish I could tell you that my smile was genuine but that would not be true.*

We have to learn how to give our best—even when the worst is being said about us. We need to keep on preaching and smiling and not react in an ungodly fashion. Like the song in the Disney movie *Frozen* where Elsa says, *Let it Go*. That's what we need to do. Forget about criticism. There's an old story that goes like this: When mud is thrown at you don't wipe it off because that's our first response. If you do, it will only get messier, so just let it dry and then it will just falls off. Good advice to live by.

Forsaken, Betrayed, and Surrounded by Incompetence

The Bible tells us, "Jesus said to him [Peter], Assuredly, I say to you that this night, before the rooster crows, you will deny Me three times. Peter said to Him, 'Even if I have to die with You, I will not deny You!' And so said all the disciples," (Matthew 26:34-35). All of the disciples—not just Peter— said, "*Lord, we'll die for You!*" But when the point of persecution came into their lives, the Bible says in that moment they all forsook Him. Every one of them abandoned Him, left Him, and deserted Him. But it got worse. Later, when Jesus was on the cross He cried out, "My God, My God, why have You forsaken Me?" (Matthew 27:46).

This was a time of great betrayal, denial, and suffering for Jesus. Even His disciples forsook Him and fled, but it was not without an eternal, emancipating purpose. The Bible says, "but all this was done that the Scriptures of the prophets might be fulfilled," (Matthew 26:56). Nobody fought for Him. Nobody stood with Him. Nobody defended Him. Nobody said, "*I've got your back,*" and at least meant it. In the moment of testing, everyone was a coward. Jesus went on doing good and giving His best anyway—while being forsaken, abandoned, deserted, and cut off. He gave unselfishly, generously, and mercifully to all that were undeserving. He continued giving even though He was rejected and denied. Jesus could have said, "*I will only give my best for those who don't forsake me or fail me,*" but He didn't.

We are all forsaken at some point. You may be forsaken by loved ones or your employer. There will be times when you will feel absolutely alone and everyone who told you, "I'm going to be there for you," will be gone—off living their own lives.

At that point what are you going to do? How are you going to act? Are you going to retaliate, respond negatively, or have a bad attitude? That happened to me when I went through a period of adversity called cancer. There were some people who didn't call or visit me anymore. And that hurt a little bit because they were friends of mine. It was never my intention to judge them, and I'm so grateful that God brought other people into my life during that season. But there will always be times when people fail to meet our expectations or abandon us in a time of need. What Jesus wants us to learn is how to give our best, continue to do good, and above all— walk in love during these times.

Recently, I was leaving the church office and saw some former employees. I nodded and smiled but they didn't acknowledge me, or say, "hi." I admit that it bothered and upset me a little, but then I heard the Holy Spirit challenge me, by saying, *why didn't you go up and say something to them?*

He put me in check, because He knew that I didn't do everything I could have done. I did not do my best. We are so quick to give less than our best in these situations, by not taking the high road. Not giving people the benefit of the doubt by initiating conversations, or taking responsibility for our own actions. Each day introduces new experiences for people as a result of bad news, not feeling well, or just having a bad day. Let's challenge ourselves to do our best when we are confronted with the issues of life via our own experiences or the experiences of others.

Not only was Jesus forsaken, He was betrayed. We know that the price on Jesus' head was 30 pieces of silver, but Judas' betrayal had begun long before that fateful night in the Garden of Gethsemane. In fact, Judas proved his disloyalty by betraying a trust as the keeper of the money bag. He had been robbing Jesus for a long time. "Now he said this, not because he cared about the poor [for he had never cared about them], but because he was a thief; and since he had the money box [serving as treasurer for the twelve disciples], he used to pilfer (steal) what was put into it," (John 12:6 AMP).

As treasurer for Jesus' ministry, Judas was entrusted with everything that was collected. It doesn't take much to imagine what type of comments might come from Judas. *"Jesus, this is wonderful that people are giving. The money we collect from the offering will help the poor and feed those who are hungry!"* But every night in secret he'd say, "one for Jesus, one for me, one for Jesus, one for me." He did this regularly and routinely. If you think about it, it really is amazing that the ministry was still able to function and have their needs met with a thief robbing from them.

Perhaps you know of someone or you personally have gone through the experience of having someone steal from you. This is something no one should go through, especially when you know the person who is stealing from you. However, in spite of Judas' actions, Jesus and the disciples were still able to go from city to city touching people's lives. The lesson we learn from this story is that we too can recover from things that have been stolen and go on to touch the lives of those around us.

In John 6:70, Jesus calls Judas "a devil." Jesus knew everything Judas was doing and would do—He fully knew the level of betrayal He would experience in the days to come. Jesus also dealt with ongoing strife that was rooted in Judas—and yet He still blessed and provided for Judas and treated him well. Amazing!

Do you have anyone in your life like that? Someone that is always questioning what you do, always operating in an undercurrent of strife? It looks like their mission in life is to create strife. It could be strife in a marriage; strife in a relationship, or strife with a close family member. It can be horribly draining—especially when it feels like all you do is fight about everything. *Why can't you just agree with me one time? Why can't you be positive instead of always negative?*

Jesus constantly had to deal with tension and undercurrents, and yet He was still able to give His best. Jesus teaches us how to be merciful even to a Judas. We will all have a Judas or two in our lives. They may rip you off or sell you out for the right price, be it a co-worker and even someone who you consider to be a close friend, someone you trust—all the while planning how to take advantage of you.

How do we deal with such betrayal? Rather than judgment and wrath, do we extend mercy or do we get even? *Don't act like you don't know what I'm talking about.* Think about what your life would be like today, if you were caught doing the things you used to do. We'd want mercy to be extended. Right?

During Jesus' earthly ministry, He was faced with multiple disappointments and frustrations. The disappointment of the Pharisees, who early in His ministry were friendly to Him, but later rejected Him. The frustration with His disciples, who seemed oblivious to who He really was; even though He had spent three and a half years teaching and training them. The repeated frustration of wondering, *Will they ever get it?* Failed attempts to heal and cast out demons; wanting to call fire down from heaven and destroy people; and the arguing among them, as to who would be the greatest. The disciples lacked humility and love for each other. The very people who should have known better, who were taught by the best teacher in the world, failed and messed up. The failures of the disciples remind us that they were people just like us, not super-spiritual people.

· ·

We can't change difficult people, but we can
change how we think and act toward them.

· ·

Many times, we can write people off that are difficult and hard to deal with—label them, ignore them, or distance ourselves from them. Most people will go to great measures to avoid conflict—whether they move away from difficult neighbors or divorce their annoying spouse or leave a church full of imperfect people.

We can't change difficult people, but we can change *how we think and act toward them.* Our decision will make the difference. It will change the atmosphere and environment so that you can be at the top of your game; and still perform even if you're in pain or injured. Meditate on this thought; Jesus lives in us every day, not just on Sunday morning!

In Pain, Suffering, and Grief

No one has known suffering in this life like Jesus did. Yet He continued to give His best and do good even though He encountered great trials and grief. We know Jesus wept over Lazarus' death. He was genuinely grieved, even though He knew Lazarus would soon be raised from the dead. He weeps, because we weep. The Bible says that Jesus *wept over* Jerusalem. He grieved over the city that would not receive His ministry because they were full of unbelief. The Bible also tells us, "Beloved, do not think it strange concerning the fiery trial which is to try you, as though some strange thing happened to you; but rejoice to the extent that you partake of Christ's sufferings, that when His glory is revealed, you may also be glad with exceeding joy," (1 Peter 4:12-13).

There are going to be tests and trials in our lives. There are going to be some losses, but despite this, we are called to rejoice in our suffering and maintain the joy of the Lord. By His example, Jesus shows us how to maintain our joy during pain and suffering. He taught us to cast our cares upon God and trust Him for the outcome. As difficult as it is, we are to continue giving our best when we're feeling our worst. We continue to be part of the family unit, we continue to show up for work, and we continue to go to church. We continue being a faithful husband, wife, father, and mother, and we continue "in our faith, grounded and steadfast and not moved away from the hope of the gospel which we have heard," (Colossians 1:23).

Jesus gave His best even while experiencing the very worst pain and suffering. "Just as many were astonished at you, so His visage (face) was marred more than any man; and His form more than the sons of men," (Isaiah 52:14). He was so disfigured that He was unrecognizable. He was grotesque to look at. Hollywood attempts to recreate what Jesus might have looked like but they can't reconstruct the real thing.

The Bible also says in Isaiah that, "He is despised and rejected by men, a man of sorrows and acquainted with grief. And we hid, as it were, our faces from Him; He was despised, and we did not esteem Him," (Isaiah 53:3). In another verse, it says, "I gave My back to those who struck Me, and My cheeks to those who plucked out the beard; I did not hide My face from shame and spitting," (Isaiah 50:6). Jesus still gave His best even though He was under extreme pain and suffering. What does this teach us? He teaches us longsuffering, endurance, and perseverance in the midst of suffering excruciating pain.

Let's be honest. Very few people will ever experience the level of pain Jesus did, in fact we couldn't and wouldn't want it. That's not to minimize the pain you're experiencing, but we need to know what to do when it happens. The Bible says, "*endure like a good soldier.*" This may seem simplistic, but the reality is that there will be times when we just have to endure—we have to push on, push through, and push beyond the pain. Bite the bullet and bear it. Have some old fashion grit, bulldog tenacity! They say the bulldog's nose is slanted backwards, so it can continue to breathe without letting go!

We've got to be what I call a good rebounder, because everyone misses shots once in a while. Not everyone will make it the first time, because opponents will try to block your shot. But you keep on pushing your way through, even though you may face someone like basketball star Dikembe Mutomo, who tries to block your shot and waves his finger in front of you saying, *no,* but then you shoot another shot. You have to rebound from your failures!

As long as we live on this earth we will experience pain. Physical pain caused by illness or emotional pain caused by relationships. Maybe you're struggling with disappointment and discouragement right now, and you feel like giving up. Don't! Keep pushing through the pain and keep going. If you fail, just get back up. That's what you do! *Get up.* That's what made Rocky Balboa in the "Rocky" movie, a great champion. He got up just one more time. "Yo Adrian, I did it!"

There's going to be a level of pain as we live for Christ, based on the choices we have to make. When you don't want to compromise, there's going to be pain. When you choose to obey God, there's going to be pain. When you refuse sin, there's going to be pain. When you don't give into temptation, there's going to be pain. When people ostracize and judge you, there's going to be pain. That's why we have to learn how to endure and be tougher than our toughest day! We have to know and believe that the persistence of God will wear down the resistance of the enemy! That's why the Bible says in Timothy, "Endure hardship as a good soldier," (2 Timothy 2:3). The Bible also compares our Christian walk to being athletes (1 Corinthians 9:26-27) and farmers (James 5:7). These scriptures will empower you with toughness and endurance in spite of your circumstances. Words like fatigue, soreness, hurt, worn out, exhausted, angry, and frustrated all come with the job. You will never be a good soldier, athlete, or farmer if you don't learn to persevere.

> When you choose to obey God,
> there's going to be pain.

Even though you're going through pain, you still have to be productive. You still have to be positive. You still have to have godly priorities. You still have to have a godly perspective. You still have to have purpose, and you still have to have praise in your life. You must persist to do God's will.

God will always help us override and supersede what we feel. No matter what's going on in our lives, it's not a time to quit or give up. Like Jesus, we can't be offended with the Judases and sceptics around us, or the Peters who deny us. We can't miss the opportunity to be a blessing to someone else because of the way we feel. Be aware that someone is always watching you; they're learning and growing from what you do or don't do, just by watching. We can't just call Him "Savior"—we must call Him "Lord," too. We must follow in the footsteps of Paul whose writings describe what our walk with Christ should look like; "I am a prisoner of the Lord Jesus Christ, I am a debtor, I am a fellow servant, I am crucified," (Ephesians 3:1, Romans 1:14, Revelation 22:9, Galatians 2:20). We can't just wear a cross around our neck. We must lift up the cross and bear the cross in our everyday life, and be the best for Christ.

Again, be tougher than your toughest day; and don't fall apart every time something bad happens or doesn't go the way you expected. We must grow our pain threshold and remember the testing of our faith produces endurance, perseverance, character and hope. Just throw another 50 pounds on the bench press and push!

CHAPTER 3

He is despised and rejected by men, a Man of sorrows and acquainted with grief. And we hid, as it were, our faces from Him; He was despised, and we did not esteem Him. Surely He has borne our griefs and carried our sorrows; yet we esteemed Him stricken, smitten by God, and afflicted.

—Isaiah 53:3-4

There are those who debate whether or not Jesus ever felt bad. They believe He was immune to our broken, mortal, human experience, and above simple emotion, unable to feel what we feel—but that could not be further from the truth. What they fail to recognize is that He was 100 percent man, too—a man that could be touched, a man who suffered, a man of sorrows. Jesus identifies with us, He "[knows exactly how it feels to be human] in every respect as we are, yet without [committing any] sin," (Hebrew 4:15b AMP).

Now maybe you are thinking, *Hey, Diego, it's wonderful to study Jesus as the example of doing good when feeling bad, and giving His best when feeling His worst, but that's Jesus, and I'm not Jesus. Jesus was God, and therefore it was much easier for Jesus to do that, and so much harder for me.* Well, the Bible blows that idea right out of the water. "For to this you were called, because Christ also suffered for us, leaving us an example, that you should follow His steps," (1 Peter 2:21)

The Word of God is not going to tell us that we have the ability to follow Christ's example if we aren't capable of it. God cannot and will not lie—that means that we absolutely have the ability to follow Christ's example. What is the level of expectation we are to live up to? Our example and model is no one else other than Jesus, "Who committed no sin, nor was deceit found in His mouth; who, when He was reviled, did not revile in return; when He suffered, He did not threaten, but committed Himself to Him who judges righteously," (1 Peter 2:22-23). Some might say, *"Well, I know someone who claimed to be a Christian and they didn't do right by me."* That might be true, but remember they are not your lord, or the one you should follow and pattern your life after. Don't make Jesus pay for someone else's failure.

No Discord

As we grow in our Christian walk, we must continue to give our best and do good to people who don't deserve it, in spite of what they do! Self-control is a fruit of the Spirit which govern us so we don't react to impulses and temptations. Feeling badly, or not liking something or someone does not give us the right to do any of the following things: complain, gossip, retaliate, get offended, or give up. *I don't like this marriage. I don't like this job. I don't like this car. I don't like this school. I should get paid more.* None of that really matters. Why? Because Jesus said, we are to follow Him and live by His example and follow in His steps.

The book of Proverbs gives us a clear picture of how God feels about specific things. "These six things the Lord hates, yes, seven are an abomination to Him: a proud look, a lying tongue, hands that shed innocent blood, a heart that devises wicked plans, feet that are swift in running to evil, a false witness who speaks lies, and one who sows discord among brethren," (Proverbs 6:16-19).

I love how this scripture is written, because it really underscores the seventh thing that God hates most—someone who sows discord among the brethren. There's more emotion attached to that one. He's serious about it! We have no business talking about anybody, because God says it's an abomination! It's absolutely unacceptable to Him.

We can't let our feelings dictate what we do. We may not be in agreement with certain believers or ministers or a leader in the body of Christ, but that doesn't give us the right to talk about them. *Christians can sometimes be the worst!* Don't go to dinner after church and start gossiping about a family everybody else is talking about. Don't tear down the pastor or tear down and gossip about your boss, company, work, spouse, or neighbors. *Let's talk about so and so.* Don't do it. It's much wiser to just bite your tongue and shut up. This is serious stuff!

Not long ago, I heard a story about three pastors who went out to lunch together. As soon as they were seated at their table, two of them started talking about another pastor who wasn't with them. After a couple of minutes of this, the third pastor stood up, turned his chair around, and sat back down with his back to them. It only took a few seconds, before the first two noticed what he had done, and then they abruptly stopped their conversation. The third pastor slowly turned back around and they said, "We apologize. We'll never do that again." Sometimes that's what you need to do to your friends, and your family, just turn your back. I promise you, they'll get the point. No matter how we feel or what has been done to us, God says, *we don't have the right to retaliate, threaten, or seek out revenge.* We don't even have the right to be offended.

More than 30 years ago, I became a youth pastor. I had a really good friend who was also in ministry. We were both young and zealous but as time went on we both got busy and drifted apart. Through the grapevine, I heard that his wife had cheated on him—with the senior pastor of the church he served at. It was devastating and caused ripples, like an earthquake, in the Kingdom of God, and my heart went out to him.

Not long ago, the Lord brought us back together and he invited me to speak at his church. It didn't take long before we were catching up on everything that had happened in our lives since we were young men. He's now remarried, and for the past 21 years his marriage has been great. But I was shocked when I ran into the former senior pastor of my friend in the green room. I was astonished, and I asked my friend, "What's *he* doing here?" He answered me and said, "Oh, he's on my staff and he works for me." I said, "He *works* for you?!" "Yeah, as a matter of fact, we all go on vacation together, the four of us, including my ex-wife. They live seven houses away from us. He and I work out together every day." I thought to myself, *Oh, my goodness!* What a great example of reconciliation and living peacefully with those who have wronged you. That's the love and grace of God personified.

Now you may be wondering, *"Pastor, do I have to do that?"* No, I'm not saying you have to do that, but you *do* have to live by God's standard. We should behave and act towards others the way Jesus did and understand that you don't have the right to be offended. Yes, you may get mad, upset, disappointed, frustrated, angry and really ticked off! But, you don't have the right to retaliate. You don't have any rights outside of God's Word. And you don't have the right to talk and gossip about others. But, you and I have are obligated to act like Jesus. Our prayer should be *"Lord, please help me, and teach me to forgive."* We must not respond to what we want, but what Christ asks of us. The reward for *avoiding discord* and *doing good* will be His blessing and favor and hearing Him say, *"well done my good and faithful servant."*

Keep Your Heart Pure

When Jesus commissioned his disciples and sent them out, He told them, "Heal the sick, cleanse the lepers, raise the dead, cast out demons. Freely you have received, freely give," (Matthew 10:8). That all sounds exciting and glorious, but

Jesus knew the disciples would encounter resistance and trouble along the way. So He gave them a protocol to follow. "And when you go into a household, greet it. If the household is worthy, let your peace come upon it. But if it is not worthy, let your peace return to you. And whoever will not receive you nor hear your words, when you depart from that house or city, shake off the dust from your feet," (Matthew 10:12-14).

Jesus never let a few bad apples spoil the bunch. He essentially said to the disciples, "*Listen, not everyone is going to receive the gospel, but you go there with a pure heart. As freely as you have received, freely give.*" Notice he didn't say, "*depending on how they treat you, will determine how you give.*" No, Jesus said, "as freely as you have received from me, freely give with the same measure." If you have only received a little from Him, give a little, but if you received generously from Him, which we all have, then give according to that measure.

Jesus never let a few bad apples spoil the bunch.

Doing what Jesus asks us to do is following in His footsteps—*I want you to heal, I want you to cast out devils, I want you to be a blessing; but if they don't want to receive the gospel, that's OK. Don't shut down and quit. Don't label everyone and get ugly! Just move on to the next town.* Be ready to give your best, not your worst because of past experiences.

Some of the bad apples Jesus encountered were Judas, the rich young ruler, the Samaritans, the Pharisees, the thief on the cross, Herod, and Pilate to name a few, but He never let them affect His actions. He continued to heal the sick. He taught about forgiveness, loving others, and being kind. Jesus gave freely of His heart, His time, His resources, and His word. He didn't allow the bad apples to stop His calling or His ministry.

I wonder how many people are in the "parked" position of life, due to the actions of others. Do they realize Jesus takes the hit for that, because they are out of commission and M.I.A.? I also wonder how many were in active ministry and service to the Lord and are now on the sidelines today, due to the past. Consequently, they're not walking in their calling or their gift as a result of a few bad apples.

How many lives would be lost today, if Jesus behaved like some Christians? Nicodemus would never have heard the good news. Peter would never have been the rock of the church. The woman caught in adultery would never have received God's forgiveness. Lazarus would never have been raised from the dead. The list goes on and on—so much would have been lost if Jesus let a few bad apples stop Him.

I remember something that happened when I was very young in ministry. I just wanted the opportunity to serve and I was very enthusiastic about giving my heart, my time, and my resources. And I believed the best of every person. I'll never forget one day, when a man walked into the church and I waited on him. He told me a hardship story, how he had lost his job and was living with his wife out of their car. He told me he had applied everywhere, but couldn't find any work. Then he threw out some names of well-known preachers. He said, "You know what? I was married by pastor so-and-so, and a member of a well-known church in Los Angeles."

He knew just the right things to tell me. Then he said, "You know what? I'm an artist, and my work isn't selling. I'll loan you my portfolio in good faith as a down payment for anything that you can give me just to show you that I'm sincere." He pulled out all these gorgeous pieces of art work. They were amazing. Then he said, "I'll sell them to you for whatever you want to give me. I just need some money for my wife and my kid." I said, "I don't want your sketches." I then reached for my wallet and pulled out $35, and for me back then, that was a lot of money. Then I went to the other assistant pastor and said, "can I borrow $20 from you?" I handed the guy $55. I was feeling really good about myself, thinking I had helped someone.

Then, not many days later, we got a phone call from another church in the area and they said, "Be on the lookout for this guy. He's a scammer." They told us his story and sure enough, it was the exact same story he told me. You talk about distrust and bitterness seeping in. I'll tell you, with the next six people that came to me with a heart-wrenching story, needless to say, I reacted with closed hands. I thought, *Oh no, I'm not falling for that one again. I'm not helping you.* If you've ever been burned, then you know how hard it can be to trust people again. Someone can be weeping in front of you, but you feel cold or indifferent. You might say, "You know what? I'm not even going to loan you a handkerchief!" You can become so desensitized.

It's unfortunate that I have felt that way because of past encounters with some churches and pastors. Whenever things seem to go in that direction, it triggered the wound within me, and I'd write them off just that quick. I had to allow God to come in and heal my heart. Let Him do the same for you—we cannot afford to allow a few bad apples to spoil our generosity or derail the gifting that God has given us. We can't afford to be on the sidelines while the game is going on. It's time for you to wear the uniform again. Lace up your shoes and get back in the game. Slide into home plate again. Why? Because the wins and losses are eternal.

Find Your Joy

There are so many people in churches today that don't dream anymore. They go through all the necessary "steps" that are supposed to make a difference in their life such as praying, believing God, confessing His Word, and fasting, but when things don't turn out the way they hoped, they believe all their effort was for nothing. They say to themselves, *why put myself out there, just to be disappointed.*

In spite of the setbacks in your life, I challenge you to keep your faith turned on. Keep expecting God to come through for you and keep believing for healings. I challenge you to believe for signs, wonders, and miracles. Keep believing for the supernatural in your life, and above all—don't let setbacks or disappointments rob you.

Jesus never let failure, lack, or setbacks stop Him from believing and expecting miracles—even when things didn't seem to be going the way they should. For example, when the disciples couldn't cast the demon out of the boy because Jesus said that kind would only come out by prayer and fasting; the disciples' lack of faith to believe that a little boy's lunch of two fish and five loaves was enough to feed 5,000 people; or when the disciples could not catch any fish and toiled all night. In spite of all the disappointments that Jesus faced, He kept believing and kept expecting God to come through. No matter how bad the scenario was, he still generated His faith and believed God.

Keep believing for the supernatural in your life,
and above all—don't let setbacks
or disappointments rob you.

How did Jesus do this? He never let His circumstances determine His joy. Jesus' joy was not hooked up to His friends, His followers, His miracles, His treasury, what He wore, where He lived, or what others said about Him. Unfortunately, that is where too many of us have our joy hooked up too—how much we earn, what kind of car is in our driveway, or how many Facebook followers we have, and how many likes we get. Jesus' joy was never dependent on things like that. He didn't rely on that "stuff."

The Bible says, "Though the fig tree may not blossom, nor fruit be on the vines; though the labor of the olive may fail, and the fields yield no food; though the flock may be cut off from the fold, and there be no herd in the stalls—yet I will rejoice in the Lord, I will joy in the God of my salvation," (Habakkuk 3:17-18). The context of this scripture is a story that goes from bad to worse to unbearable. *Nothing* is working—but there is that little word in the verse, yet. *Yet, I will rejoice in the Lord.* Not after, not when things change, not when the miracle shows up, but *now.* He says, *"Even when everything is bad, I will keep my joy. I'll keep praising God."*

There's a pastor by the name of Jack Hinton who went to a leper colony in Tobago, Trinidad. He was leading praise and worship in a service there, when he noticed one lady whose back was turned to him the entire time. Toward the end of praise and worship, he asked if anyone had any requests. Hearing that question, the lady turned around and he was overwhelmed by what he saw. She had no nose, and he could see her insides. The leprosy had distorted her physical form. She had no ears. They'd withered away, along with all her fingers—all she had were palms.

When she raised her hand, he pointed at her and said, "Yes, ma'am." She said, "Would you sing the song, *Count Your Many Blessings, Number them One by One?*" Pastor Jack was so moved he began to cry, and they had to usher him off the stage as someone came out and finished the song. Afterward, a friend came to him and said, "You'll probably never sing that song again." Pastor Jack answered, "Oh, I will sing it again. I just will never sing it the same way that I sang it before!"

If that woman could find joy to count all of her blessings regardless of her circumstances, how much more should we? Where does our joy come from? Luke says, our joy comes knowing that our name is written in the Lamb's book of life (Luke 10:20). We need to remember that every day! Our joy is not hooked up to the latest fads, our retirement portfolio, where we work, or our money. Our joy is hooked up to the fact that heaven is our home!

Heaven rejoices when someone is saved. Even the angels rejoice! (Luke 15:10) Scripture teaches us that, *Weeping endures for the night, but joy comes in the morning. All things work together for our good. What the devil meant for evil, God will turn it for good. His grace is sufficient. Be confident in this thing that He who has begun a good work in you will complete it.* These verses bring me joy and comfort no matter what I'm going through! (Psalm 30:5, Romans 8:28, Genesis 50:20, 2 Corinthians 12:9, Philippians 1:6)

Joy also comes through true Christian relationships that we have in our lives—wonderful invested friendships; the brotherhood; the saints bring us joy. Last of all, joy should come in knowing that no matter what things look like, God is in control. Right now, our world looks like everything is out of control. But someone once said, *"God is on the throne large and in charge."*

Have you ever thought about all the questions you can't wait to ask God, when you get to heaven? All of the wrongs, hurts, misunderstandings, and the whys? You know what? When you get to heaven, I don't believe you are going to remember those questions anymore because they won't matter! All those doubts and questions will disappear, because when you walk through the pearly gates, when you walk on streets of gold, when you see diamonds sparkling on the walls, and when you see the glory and the presence of the Lord, nothing else will seem as important as the joy of finally being home. It will be one of those *forget about everything else* moments.

The Secret to Overcome

Jesus had every right to be selfish and to think only about Himself. Instead, Jesus demonstrated pure selflessness. Paul followed His example, which we see in his writings to the Philippians: "For I am hard-pressed between the two, having a desire to depart and be with Christ, which is far better. Nevertheless to remain in the flesh is more needful for you," (Philippians 1:23-24).

What is Paul saying? *If I had my choice, I would go to heaven. I want to die. I'm an old man now. I've suffered a lot. It's taken its toll on my life. But as I look at the Church, the Church still needs my influence. It still needs my gift. I'm going to do what is best for others rather than what is best for me.*

Here's what I want you to understand: to live a selfless life you have to be able to think about others and connect with them. The man who keeps himself busy helping people with needs greater than his own doesn't have time to envy people who have more than he does.

When you're hurting, go find someone to minister to.
It breaks the bonds of self-pity.

One of the most dangerous things that we can do when we're in pain is to withdraw and isolate ourselves. I see it all the time. Suddenly, they disappear when they are going through hard times. Like Houdini the magician. Poof! They are gone and nowhere to be found. You can't find them anywhere. They're M.I.A. and A.W.O.L. during a critical time when they most need the support and strength of the body of believers, friends, and family.

When you're hurting, go find someone to minister to. It breaks the bonds of self-pity. It breaks the chains of depression and discouragement. Keep yourself busy when you're going through times of pain. Keep *doing good*—stay connected to others and turn the tables on the devil. *You hurt me; I'm going to make you regret it!* Find a need and go minister to it, and I promise you the depression, discouragement, and pain in your life won't seem as relevant anymore. It will lose its power over you.

Do you know someone who is allergic to peanuts? It can be very serious—often life threatening. Some people can't even be in the same room with them. They could ingest just 1/100th percent of a peanut and die from it. One current medical treatment that is being offered involves giving the patient 1/1000th percent of a peanut and gradually increasing the amount over weeks and months until they can eat a whole peanut. This process helps the patient build up their tolerance toward something that was deadly to them before.

This same principle applies to us, too. We need to start building our tolerance toward things that we couldn't stand and were harmful to us. We start with the little things, giving and doing good; changing our reactions and responses, and gradually over time we learn to have victory to conquer the big things.

What do we do if the worst case scenario happens? You and I need to be prepared the same way Jesus was prepared, when the people didn't receive Him. "Now He could do no mighty work there, except that He laid His hands on a few sick people and healed them. And He marveled because of their unbelief. Then He went about the villages in a circuit, teaching," (Mark 6:5-6).

When Jesus went to His hometown called Nazareth, the power of the Lord was present to heal, to teach and to do miracles. The Bible says *He could do virtually nothing because of their unbelief.* So how did Jesus handle this unexpected situation? Perhaps He thought to himself, *I know what I'll do. I'm going to go teach. I'm going to go build their faith. I'm going to try to change their way of thinking, instead of giving up on them.*

It's amazing how many Christians are unprepared for the worst case scenarios in their life. What are you going to do when someone offends you? What are you going to do when your teenagers go wayward, or your marriage falls apart? What are you going to do if you lose your job? I pray it doesn't happen to you, but what if it does?

Don't fight, don't panic, and don't complain about the circumstance. You overcame a struggle or conflict in your past through the help of God, so you will overcome this one too. Just relax, rest, stay calm, and you will overcome! Some things you're never going to be able to change. I'm sorry to tell you, but you may never be able to change your spouse or your neighbor or your boss. So how do we handle situations that you just can't change? You just learn to overcome it, by trusting God one day at a time.

> There are so many people who are
> being hit by the riptides of life,
> and are drowning spiritually.

Many years ago, I was in Huntington Beach and I got hit by a wave called a riptide. It took me under. I almost drowned because I fought so hard against it. I didn't realize then, that the worst thing you can do, is to go into a panic mode. Experts say if you're ever caught, just relax. It will eventually bring you back up. But I fought against it and it made it worse.

There are so many people who are being hit by the riptides of life, and are drowning spiritually. They need to learn to relax and trust God and not panic so when the tide turns it will bring them back to the shoreline. If your spouse or your kids are acting crazy, stay in faith. Accept that there will be times when things won't change or go as planned. Some things aren't fair and unfortunately you will get hurt. People are people, and they're frail. That's life, so be prepared now. *Well, I'm confessing and believing that will never happen to me.* Well, all I can say is, I hope it doesn't, but stuff happens to everybody. People will say, *I was the most qualified for this job, and I didn't get it!* Things aren't fair in this world, but you still have the promises of God. *Well, I thought that person would never treat me that way.* My friend, that's the nature of some people.

The question is, how do you give your best when feeling your worst—and do good when feeling bad—and move forward when circumstances are pushing you back? According to 1 Corinthians 13:13, we do it by faith, by hope, and by love. These are the three most powerful truths that keep us moving forward. *By faith* is who I believe in. *By hope* is how I believe. By *love* is why I believe.

Bottom line, you're going to give your best because you have faith in God. You are going to give your best because you hope in God, and you are going to give your best because you love God. Only complete devotion to Christ will allow you to override how you are feeling.

There's a story told of King Cyrus, who reigned over the Persian Empire. He had just conquered a prince, his wife, and kids from a foreign land. King Cyrus had the prince and his family brought before him. The King of Persia looked at the prince and asked, "What will you give me if I release you?" The prince answered, "I'll give you half of my kingdom." The King replied, what will you give me if I release your children?" The prince said, "I'll give you my entire kingdom." Then the King asked, "What will you give me if I release your wife?" The prince answered, "You can take my life. I'll die."

The king was so moved by the response that he released the prince, his wife, and his kids. As they were traveling back to their homeland, the prince looked at his wife and said,

"Wasn't King Cyrus a very handsome, kind, and generous man?" She looked at him out of love, devotion, and respect and said, "I never noticed because my eyes were fixed upon you." Only what you do for Christ out of your deep devotion, commitment, and love for Him will stand. Everything else will end, so keep your eyes fixed on Jesus.

....

Only what you do for Christ out of your deep devotion,
commitment, and love for Him will stand.

....

In the story of King David, we see how he reacted when His child that he had with Bathsheba died. The Bible says he went to the temple and worshipped God. "So David arose from the ground, washed and anointed himself, and changed his clothes; and he went into the house of the Lord and worshiped. Then he went to his own house; and when he requested, they set food before him, and he ate," (2 Samuel 12:20). Soon after they got pregnant again and had Solomon, a great King. Why? Because of faith, hope, and love. They didn't give up!

Another story when faith was challenged is that of John the Baptist, when he was in prison and soon to be beheaded by Herod. John sent his followers to ask Jesus, "Are you truly the Messiah or do we look for another?" The loud screaming words of doubt in John's head were trying to get him to question whether Jesus was the Messiah. This is the same John that just a short time earlier was heard proclaiming His faith in Jesus as the Savior of the world with his declaration, *"Behold the*

Lamb of God." In the prison of darkness, alone, hungry, and tired, doubt will rise in all of us and the pain of our circumstance screams loudly with echoes of doubt. The response that Jesus gave John, gets him past his pain, to the revelation that he lived, to fulfill his purpose. Jesus said, "Tell John all that you've heard and seen; the blind see, the lame walk, the deaf can hear and the dead are raised," (Matthew 11:4-5).

When pain is trying to control and dictate to you, that you are something you are not, and fill you with doubt, *refuse* to listen to what your feelings are saying. Instead, rehearse God's faithfulness, boast in God, and talk about the bigness of your God. Move forward and fulfill your purpose.

Application

So, how to do good? How to give your best? "And whatever you do, do it heartily, as to the Lord and not to men, knowing that from the Lord you will receive the reward of the inheritance; for you serve the Lord Christ," (Colossians 3:23-24). When we do good and give our best, we must keep in mind that we are doing it for the Lord and not for man. If our intention for doing good is to receive acknowledgement and encouragement only from man, we are doing it for the wrong reasons. Everyone loves a thank you, good job, or a high five but what happens when you don't get that response? The answer is, keep doing good and give your best anyway because Jesus is watching and listening. Whatever we do should always be to please and serve the Lord. That shows our gratitude for what He has done for us.

I remember one time, when I was entering a store, I opened the door and paused. Within a few seconds, a complete stranger walked right past me into the store; and they didn't even acknowledge me with a *thank you*. Of course, I said to myself, *how rude, here I am holding the door open and not even* a *thank you*. Needless to say, for a split second my thoughts went from being nice to thinking, *I should have released the door and let it slam right on the person*. Ouch! (Just kidding.) This reminds me of how fast my attitude went from good to bad.

At that very moment, the Lord dropped a thought in my mind saying, *who are you holding the door open for, Me or them? Who are you doing it for, Me or them? Would you like the "thank you" or "reward" to come from Me or them?* Doing good is not based on how we feel. Feelings can fluctuate, because I know mine do. They're like the wind and politics. Regardless of whether we're upset, frustrated, disappointed, fearful, alone, rejected, or discouraged, I must give my best. Too much is riding on our life to be led, governed, and influenced by our moods, feelings, and emotions. We must keep our eyes off people and keep our eyes on Jesus—so we can continue to *do good* in spite of how we feel on the inside or what is going on around us on the outside.

Recently, I was hosting a Christmas party at a restaurant. I reserved the patio for my guests, or so I thought. When I got there, I found out only half the patio was reserved for us, therefore, we would be sharing the space with the public. I was disappointed, and somewhat upset, because I planned on saying a few words, and possibly a little sermon (can't you imagine a night without me speaking). Huh! I left the restaurant for a couple of minutes to cool down, when the thought came to me, *Get over it. So what! Go back in there and enjoy the evening even though you're disappointed. Put your game face on and go have fun!* Well, I did just that. Even though we experience disappointment, we must push through *to do good* and *give our best.* Remember, Jesus is our model. He will reward you, and He is the one you want to please, right?

To achieve our goal, it's going to take understanding and certain actions on our part. We must apply the skills we need to be successful. Don't become discouraged if you don't get it the first time—remember Rome wasn't built in a day. It's my hope that as you take the first steps of examining and learning some key principles, you will be encouraged and grow in mastering the art of doing good and being your best. Let's begin.

Perspective

Have the right perspective in front of you, knowing that what you are feeling won't last. Remember, someone is always watching you and they can be affected by your actions. The person you think you are right now, is not really who you are. Jesus said, *I always do those things that please my Father and I came not to do my will but the will of my Father,* (John 8:29b, John 6:38). It's about always doing everything as unto the Lord so that's why we give our best.

Have you ever considered the possibility that these behaviors and feelings have not always been a part of you? Ask yourself, *are my actions presently planting the kind of seeds that I want to reap, knowing the seed I sow, will be the seed I reap? Is my behavior starting to reshape my personality with traits of excuses, complaining, denial, victimizing, and blaming? Are my reactions to situations better or worse? Are they helping or hurting, building or destroying, advancing or hindering others?*

Jesus had a great perspective. A perspective that asks, *is what I'm feeling and going through temporal and momentary? Does it have an eternal purpose? Then we must affirm our faith by saying, there will be an end to this, and I will believe for a better ending. This is not a box office movie from Hollywood, with a sad ending. It's not over until God says it's over!*

Friends and Relationships

Interacting with people we know during difficult times helps to strengthen and encourage us. Here's what I know—we can't go through difficulties alone. We need to recruit and develop a *Dream Team;* people to pull us and push us through the barriers of life. We need people who aren't afraid to *correct us,* and *check us* when we are not doing the right thing. We all have blind spots, and sometimes we need *help to* see. When we drive our cars we depend on the rear view mirror or camera to help us see what's behind us. There are some obstacles, big and small, that we can't see without some assistance. These obstacles can cause a potential accident and bring harm into our lives. That's why we need another set of eyes to watch our backs. Isaiah 58:8b reads, "The glory of the Lord shall be your rear guard."

CHAPTER 3

....

We all have blind spots,

and sometimes we need *help* to see.

....

Everyone gets discouraged, even if a person is wearing a yellow smiley face sticker or T-shirt. That's a joke! Knowing people who have successfully made it through difficult or similar situations, can be a great inspiration. True friends will encourage and sometimes correct us because they have the advantage and can see things we can't. When I was diagnosed with terminal stage 4 cancer in 2008, there were many times that I drew on the stories of people who triumphed and were victorious over illnesses. I would repeatedly say to myself, *God's not a respecter of persons. If He healed so-and-so, I know I also will be healed.* Hundreds and hundreds of times I had to say that to encourage myself! Your story may be about illness, a financial story, a marital story or a job related story, but there's a story for you to draw strength from. In the Bible, we see stories of people who needed someone to help and encourage them during their trials. David needed Jonathan, Moses needed Aaron, Naomi needed Ruth, Paul needed Timothy, and Jesus asked Peter, James, and John to pray with Him in his hour of need. How about you?

Our Will

The will to do good is a powerful force that cannot be ignored or downplayed. Our thoughts and our minds will be influenced by what we mediate on. "Casting down arguments and every high thing that exalts itself against the knowledge of God, bringing every thought into captivity to the obedience of Christ," (2 Corinthians 10:5). Philippians 2:5 says, "Let this mind be in you which was also in Christ Jesus." God has given us a *free will* to choose. When you come to terms with your *will* and you decide *to do good* and *give your best,* that's what I call *willpower.* The Bible tells us to count the cost in Luke 14:28. That means we must exercise the necessary *energy and strength it will take to put forth the right* attitude and action. No matter what, you must determine to not stop and do whatever it takes to accomplish the goal set before you. I'm reminded of the story The Little Train That Could. The little train said, *I think I can, I think I can . . .* so he did.

Another example of mind over matter was when I changed my diet during the cancer attack to organic, healthy, raw, and clean eating. It wasn't easy—it was hard. I was accustomed to eating certain foods, desserts, and drinks that were not good for me. With God's help, I applied *mind over matter* and I stopped eating the bad food and started to force myself to like healthy food. Now after many years, it's become a lifestyle habit and I've seen the benefits. I wouldn't even think about going back.

I once read a survey about people who had survived major crises' in their life to see what similar traits they all possessed. First, they had a strong *will* to live. Secondly, they were *willing* to do whatever it took to live. That's pretty powerful. Your *will* is the choice you make and no one but you can control your *will.* You have to want it. Remember, you can lead a horse to water but you can't make him drink. In Luke 22:42 Jesus said, "Father, yet not my will, but yours be done."

Jesus put *his will* aside and chose to do the *will of the Father* on his way to the cross. He redeemed us and shed His blood for the sins of mankind. We must exercise the right *will* in our lives by what we confess and speak. We must *will* to speak the right words, *will* to give our best and *will* to do good. "Do not conform to the pattern of this world, but be transformed by the renewing of your mind. Then you will be able to test and approve what God's will is—his good, pleasing and perfect will," (Romans 12:2 NIV).

Visualize

Visualizing, and using your imagination in a good way, is living out something in your mind and your thoughts before it takes place. It's envisioning your thought first before acting it out. You can use your imagination to do your best when feeling your worst.

- See yourself smiling instead of frowning.
- See yourself laughing instead of crying.
- See yourself engaging rather than retreating.
- See yourself acting your best every day, towards your family, coworkers and friends.

It's the ability to see *good* and see the *best*, regardless of the circumstances. It's the ability to see beyond the pressures and temptations, and the ability to see yourself overcoming and conquering every negative situation in your life.

The Holy Spirit—The Helper

When we *pray* and ask the Holy Spirit to help us to do well, this becomes a huge advantage to our success. John 14:26 says, "The Holy Spirit is our helper and teacher." We are all familiar with personal trainers, coaches, mentors, and counselors. These professions help people to achieve desired results. Well, it's the same with the Holy Spirit. His job is to help you do right.

If you don't know how to do something, the Holy Spirit will help you. If you don't know where to go, He will guide you. He helps us do our best in all areas of struggle, impossibilities, and difficulties of life and there's no monthly fee. His services are free. It's all been paid for by Jesus. When you sign up to be a Christian and invite Jesus Christ to be your Lord and Savior, the Holy Spirit comes to live in you. "Or do you not know that your body is the temple of the Holy Spirit who is in you, whom you have from God, and you are not your own? For you were bought at a price; therefore glorify God in your body and in your spirit, which are God's," (1 Corinthian 6:19-20).

Even if you are struggling to do good in the midst of doing your worst, don't get discouraged. Just ask the Holy Spirit to help you, and He will, quicker than quick! He knows you better than anyone else and He can help you to do better. He's the perfect coach.

CHAPTER 3

Honesty

There's a statement that goes something like this: *if there is no self-awareness in our life, it leads to self-deception.* In other words, you need to be honest with yourself. What does doing bad and giving your worst look like for you, so you can confront and stop it? We've spent a lot of time discovering how to do good and give our best. Sometimes to accomplish this we must stop pretending and ignoring what is stopping, hindering, robbing, or plaguing us. Looking in a mirror and taking a 360 degree introspective look at yourself isn't easy or fun, but it is necessary. Ask yourself, *what do I have to change, eliminate, deny, crucify, or silence in my life?* This is a difficult but crucial question to ask.

No one can do it for you, you must decide for yourself. The Bible tells us to: Examine ourselves to see whether we are in faith (2 Corinthians 13:5); But each one must examine his own work (Galatians 6:4); But a man must examine himself (1 Corinthians 11:28). We must rid ourselves of excuses. We need to stop procrastinating, blaming, complaining, and feeling like a victim. You can't continue to justify your actions, live in fear, have negative thoughts, and be ruled by anger and strife. Stop being easily offended, easily discouraged, and wanting to quit and give up. The devil attacks and uses these weapons to stop you from doing good and giving your best. Remember, the Greater One, God Almighty, lives in you and He wants to help you meet every challenge and change your future. So let's get rid of all the stop signs, the obstacles, and the thieves in our lives. When we do this each and every day, we will make honesty a reality in our life.

....

Remember, the Greater One, God Almighty,
lives in you and He wants to help you meet
every challenge and change your future.

....

Authority

Staying under the authority of God, His Word, His Will, and His Ways, is sometimes a hard pill to swallow. Ask yourself, *do I have the authority and the right to do whatever I want?* The answer is obvious—*not as a Christ follower.* Jesus said in John 6:38 that He did not come to do His will but the will of His Father. Does this mean we should just ignore this scripture? Absolutely not! No matter what our circumstance, situation, or condition is, as Christians, we know our lives are not our own. Our lives are for His service, His purpose, and His glory! God has a purpose, plan, and will for every part of our life. Everything I do, everywhere I go, I do to honor Him. This means I live by a higher standard than myself. God uses the Bible and the Holy Spirit to tap into my conscience and direct my actions. I've learned how to submit and be brought under the governing authority of God Almighty, through His Word. As I listen to the Holy Spirit I'm able to turn away from my former passions and choices that controlled my selfish desires, cravings, and impulses.

Back in the 90s, four letters became very popular in Christendom: "WWJD." We wore T-shirts and bracelets with these letters; books were written and stickers were everywhere. Maybe you have a *What Would Jesus Do* tattoo. Back then we thought it was a pretty good slogan to live by and I believe it's still a good standard today. What would Jesus do is a good talking point, a good question, a good response to everything. So as Christ followers we have to learn to live by Galatians 2:20, "I have been crucified with Christ; it is no longer I who live, but Christ lives in me; and the life which I now live in the flesh I live by faith in the Son of God, who loved me and gave Himself for me."

Persistence

It has been said that through persistence, the snail made it onto Noah's Ark. If you climb Mount Everest, which is more than 29,000 feet, it's going to take persistence. If you had a hall of fame record it wouldn't be based only on a great play, a great game, or a great season, it would be based on a great career. That's persistence. How many times did Thomas Edison, Abe Lincoln, and even Colonel Harland Sanders of KFC fail before they were successful? We need to have the mindset, attitude, and toughness to do good, and give our best even though we fail and feel our worst. It takes good old fashioned persistence, together with the standard of doing good, and giving our best when we want to quit, give up, stop, abort, and walk away.

Persistence is a practice. Persistence is a discipline. Persistence is learned, and becomes a habit. It needs to be developed every day. It's doing it again and again, over and over, and not something we try or attempt for a while. Persistence should be controlled by the Holy Spirit, influenced by Jesus, and regulated by God. It doesn't hesitate, or delay or procrastinate. It's not fearful, indecisive, doubtful, evasive, or silent. *Persistence says I can, I will, I shall.* Persistence says, I have and I will be successful.

....

Persistence is learned, and becomes a habit.

....

I know this was a lengthy description but I think you got the point. *Persistence wears down the resistance of opposers, hindrances, obstacles, and opposition.* Remember—the persistence of dripping water can break a stone in half. This principle is taught throughout the Bible.

- Jesus prayed in the Garden of Gethsemane three times.
- Jesus was in the wilderness being tempted by the devil and He said "It is written" three times.
- Jesus laid hands on the blind man from Bethsaida two times.
- Elijah told the servant to go to the sea and look seven times before the rain came.
- Elijah laid on the dead boy three times before he came to life.
- Elijah laid on the child of the Shulamite woman two times before he came to life.
- Blind Bartemaeus cried out to Jesus repeatedly.

Patience

It is said that patience is a virtue. We need to apply and master the fruit of patience to be able to do good and give our best. Today's world is filled with stresses, deadlines, and demands. We rush here and there which creates frustration and impatience in us. It breeds and exposes an ugly part of us, which gives life to the worst part within and causes us to do badly. The Bible challenges us to be slow to anger, to be long suffering with people, and to be content. This can be hard when you are boxed in traffic, stuck in a long line, waiting for an appointment that is taking longer than you thought, or when your wife takes forever to get ready. But patience is the key that unlocks the ability for you to do good and be your best.

Learn not to be so anxious, irritable, upset, or easily frustrated. Be like Jesus—cool, calm, and collected. Don't let them see you sweat, and don't sweat the small stuff. There was a song called, *Don't Worry, Be Happy*. Patience is the byproduct of spending quality time with God. Hebrews 6:12 warns us not to become sluggish, but imitate those who through faith and patience inherit the promises. Through patience we get our inheritance. Let's be patient with ourselves. The principle of giving our best will take time to master.

Obedience

The definition of obedience is "to hear God's Word and act accordingly." Obedience is just simply doing what *Jesus asks you to do.* The Bible says, "If you love Me, keep my commandments," (John 14:15), which simply means "obey Me."

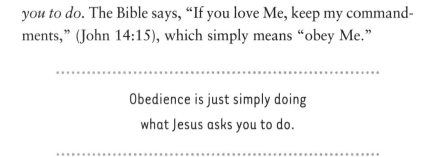

Obedience is just simply doing
what Jesus asks you to do.

As Christ-followers, we need to think in terms of getting God's permission through His Word. When we are living in obedience to Christ, we live with the understanding that we wait for His stamp of approval instead of just doing it. Remember, when you were a child you probably got in trouble because you didn't get your parent's permission. When a plane takes off or lands it needs permission or clearance from the airport tower. I remember when we were building our 47 million dollar church on 30 acres of land. The general contractor, whose name was Jack, flew me in his helicopter over the property to get an aerial view of the project. When we got aboard, he called the nearest airport to ask permission and get clearance to lift off. Now, I thought because he owned his own helicopter, he didn't need to get permission. I didn't know that he couldn't take off without it. Through this experience, I learned that Jack's obedience in following the flight policy kept us safe.

A signal on a street corner is actually an example of *getting permission*. A green light is "yes" and a red light is "no." What would happen if you ran a red light? You'd get a ticket, busted, or a fine and probably cause a bad accident. An untamed dog can cause trouble, but a trained dog will wait for his owner to give him permission as he follows a command.

Let's make sure we obey, get clearance and permission to do what we should do in our actions, attitudes, words, and thoughts. If you're actions include jealousy, unforgiveness, being ugly, or selfishness, you probably didn't get God's permission.

A few helpful thoughts:

- Will doing the opposite of what you feel or think, be a good thing for you, or not?
- Do the opposite of what your flesh wants to do.
- Do the opposite of what you feel like doing.
- Do the opposite of what the devil is telling you to do.
- Do the opposite of what people deserve.
- Do the opposite of what you normally do.
- When you are at the crossroads of negative emotions, do the opposite.
- When you are at the intersection of a negative decision, do the opposite.
- When you are at a crossroad of a negative choice, do the opposite.

Just do life instead of death, do hope instead of negativity, do peace instead of anger, do love instead of hurting, do encouragement instead of complaining, and do forgiveness instead of bitterness. God alone should be all the motivation you need to be your best.

Wisdom

To do good and give our best requires wisdom. Wisdom gives us the ability to know what to do and when to do it. Wisdom aids in our ability to make good, rational, and well-thought-out decisions. The ability to discern God's will in any situation takes wisdom. Knowing the benefits of what wisdom provides, you may be saying to yourself, *I definitely need wisdom. How do I get it?* The Bible says, "If any of you lacks wisdom, you should ask God, who gives generously to all without finding fault, and it will be given to you," (James 1:5 NIV). It's that simple, just ask God and He will give wisdom to you generously.

Wisdom helps us to see through a situation and discern the truth. Wisdom's leading will help us to recognize right from wrong. That leading will help us know what we should do and how to handle tough, difficult, and perplexing circumstances. I believe we can all agree that our life will be better off by making right decisions.

It's that simple, just ask God and
He will give wisdom to you generously.

"Be very careful, then, how you live—not as unwise but as wise, making the most of every opportunity, because the days are evil," (Ephesians 5:15-16 NIV). Making the right or wrong decision with our finances can affect our outcome. For example, borrowing, saving, spending, and loaning money. "I will instruct you and teach you in the way you should go; I will counsel you with my loving eye on you," (Psalm 32:8 NIV). Wisdom will teach you.

We might need wisdom concerning a bad relationship that may need to end. Wisdom is needed in an unhealthy marriage, where a spouse is abusive and there needs to be a season of separation, for God to work on the relationship. Wisdom is really needed when there is an unruly teenager who doesn't respect the rules of the home and is influencing a younger sibling.

Wisdom is needed when you are trying to decide whether or not you should go to a certain place that could be tempting for you. Dating someone that you know is not right for you because of your Christian walk, is when you will definitely need wisdom. It may be knowing when to speak up or when to keep your mouth shut. "The mouths of the righteous utter wisdom, and their tongues speak what is just," (Psalm 37:30 NIV). Jesus knew people, so He protected Himself with wisdom. John 2:24-25 says, "But Jesus did not commit Himself to them, because He knew all men, and had no need that anyone should testify of man, for He knew what was in man." Jesus also knew people wanted to hurt and harm Him. He wasn't ignorant or naïve; He avoided it with wisdom. John 10:39 says, "Therefore, they sought again to seize Him, but He escaped out of their hand."

"Do not forsake wisdom, and she will protect you; love her, and she will watch over you. The beginning of wisdom is this: Get wisdom. Though it cost all you have, get understanding," (Proverbs 4:6-7 NIV). Wisdom will show you how to wait on something rather than react hastily. Wisdom asks: "What and who do you need to avoid that will cause you problems and heartache?" Wisdom also asks, "Is there any area of your life where you are being neglectful, lazy, procrastinating, or foolish?" Wisdom will keep you from repeating the same mistakes over and over, and give you the patience to wait, rather than reacting hastily. When you understand the wisdom of God, you will cherish and protect your heart against anything that opposes His will for your life.

CHAPTER 4

"But I say to you, love your enemies, bless those who curse
you, do good to those who hate you, and pray for those who
spitefully use you and persecute you."

—Matthew 5:44

Doing good, independent of circumstances, environment,
conditions or the situation you are in, releases God's blessings
in your life. Do good regardless of how you feel. Make up
your mind and let it become your lifestyle—*how you live, how
you act, how you respond.* Doing good is a great witness to
people at your workplace, home, church, and gathering place.
It gets their attention. Doing good can be seen by just picking
up after yourself, or picking up a simple piece of trash. How
I talk and treat people speaks volumes. Friendliness and kindness go a long way. Letting someone cut in line in front of you,
holding open a door for someone, complimenting someone
for an achievement or just to encourage them is Jesus in
action. He is exemplified in your morals, integrity, values,
beliefs, ethics, behavior, and deeds. He is seen in how we talk

and treat people with respect, and how we value them with care and appreciation.

Jesus walked around leaving a trail of good by healing people, performing miracles, speaking life with His words, His touch, and His love.

- He did good to children who wanted to be around Him, and explained to the rich young ruler, how he could inherit eternal life.
- He did good to the woman at the well who was rejected, and visited the home of Zacchaeus, the tax collector.
- He did good to the woman caught in adultery, by not condemning her, and responded to His mother's request at the wedding in Cana.
- He did good to the hungry; the sick, the demonic; and the thief on the cross, who got saved minutes before his death.
- He did good when he told his disciple John, the one He loved, *behold your mother!*
- He did good to Malchus, when he healed his ear after it was cut off, and gave Peter a second chance after he denied knowing Jesus.
- He did good to Lazarus, by raising him from the dead; by freeing Mary Magdalene, who had many demons, and by setting free the lunatic man.

We must bring the good news to those who are deceived and are acting like the devil through their actions and lifestyle. John 10:10 says, "the thief (Satan) does not come except to steal, and to kill, and to destroy. I have come that they may have life, and that they may have it more abundantly." When we see stealing, killing, and destruction in people's lives, this is evidence that the enemy is actively at work. We need to do good by sharing and living the gospel before them, by praying even when we think they don't deserve it. We do good when we bring healing to the whole spirit, soul, and body.

Jesus is the perfect model for us to follow: "*Jesus went about doing good and healing all who were oppressed of the devil. . . .*" This verse bears repeating as it teaches us what doing good "looks like." Doing good is to bring healing to people who are sick, angry, confused, selfish, depressed, deceived, and oppressed. Doing good brings healing to the broken and forgotten people of this world.

At the beginning of this chapter, John 5:38 is quoted. The last five words of this verse states, "*For God was with Him.*" This is the secret as to how Jesus was able to do good and give His best. Wow, this is good news because *God lives in us too!* "Guard the good deposit that was entrusted to you—guard it with the help of the Holy Spirit who lives in us," (2 Timothy 1:14). God Almighty, God all powerful, the Great I Am—lives in you and brings support, encouragement, strength, and power. He also helps you to do what's difficult. At times it feels impossible and exhausting. It's not fun to do the uncomfortable and tough things. But God not only wants us to know we're loved, favored, and blessed; He also wants us to know that he has equipped us to do the work He sends us to do. Knowing this means you can give your best no matter what.

....

God Almighty, God all powerful, the Great I Am—
lives in you and brings support,
encouragement, strength, and power.

....

Doing good or giving your best when you don't want to is a must or change will never happen; heartache and frustration will be our future and the future of our society and our world. We need to teach our children this principle early and we must live it out ourselves. If you don't feel like doing good by going to work or not being a good spouse or parent, what will be the result? If you don't take care of your health, sleep, exercise, and eat right, what will be the result? If you don't study and do homework, or save money for retirement, what will be the result? I think the message is pretty clear.

In Luke 6:9, Jesus asks a question, "I will ask you one thing: Is it lawful on the Sabbath to do good or to do evil, to save life or to destroy?" Mark 3:4 says, "but they kept silent." This question is applicable to us today, "Is it lawful to do good or to do evil, to save life or to destroy or *do we remain silent?*" I believe we would agree that it's better to do good than to do evil.

Jesus challenged the system at a time when people were limited and restricted to doing things based on the law, traditions, and customs. But He did not allow the limitations imposed by the law and traditions to keep Him from doing good on the Sabbath. The question we all have to ask ourselves is *what is your Sabbath?* What holds you back?

What restricts you and keeps you silent from doing good and giving your best at all times, everywhere and with everyone?

In Conclusion

What the world, our families, marriages, friendships, churches, and jobs need, is for us to give our best when circumstances in our lives are the worst. Jesus is our supreme example of how to navigate our lives through bad feelings and bad emotions. We need to rise above them and be examples to others and fulfill the *will* of our Father. I love Jesus, because He never made excuses why He couldn't. He never said, "*I can't because of the lack of support, encouragement, and help.*" He never said, "*I won't because people are mean, ugly, and they lack kindness, appreciation, and they don't say thank you.*" Jesus never said, "*that is enough, I've had it, no more, don't bother me, I'm not available, don't disturb me.*"

Jesus' life is an expression of *grace*, by *giving* us what we don't deserve. He treats us in a way that we can't repay, bestowing on us an overabundance of kindness, gentleness, caring, and love—no matter what! I really believe we can live a happier, peaceful, more joyous and fulfilled life by the epic traits of Jesus' life in our world today. We must refuse to be controlled or driven by our surroundings and emotions; instead we must choose to give our best when we're feeling our worst. We can use this as an opportunity to do good when feeling bad and be the conduit that God will use to witness to an unsaved world. It will take work and we will be tested by trial and error, but it's worth it. It is possible to master giving your best when feeling your worst.

Right now, as I finish writing this book, I'm on an airplane. Two kids behind me are screaming and kicking my chair, and the parents don't seem to care. In my mind I'm thinking, *how inconsiderate,* but you know what, I have to practice what I preach and practice what I have written about. I have to do good and give my best no matter what. *Join me on the journey!*

My prayer for everyone reading this book is that the Lord Jesus will infuse you with understanding and patience, as you put into practice "being good and doing good" everywhere you go and with everyone you meet. Let's go make this world a better place by being living examples of what Jesus practiced, preached, and how He lived.

STUDY GUIDE

Chapter 1

1. Describe an incident where you pushed beyond your pain threshold, in spite of the emotional pain.

2. Is it possible to do our best even though we are experiencing deep levels of pain? Explain.

3. How will you let what happened or what is happening to you affect and change you? List some steps.

4. Have you allowed the hardships in your life to become excuses for bad behavior and stopped you from doing good? List some examples.

5. Jesus shows us what to do when we experience loss. He retreats to be alone with the Father. Why do you think Jesus did this?

6. Is there ever a time for us to be selfish and say, don't bother me? Explain.

7. Have you ever been troubled in spirit because you knew someone close to you betrayed you?

8. How difficult would it be for you to do good to someone who has not been good to you?

9. Have you ever asked for help from a trusted friend and they failed to come through? How did you respond?

10. How difficult is it for you to remain in total control when you are in the middle of a crisis moment?

11. How important is it to know the Word of God in times of temptation?

12. Will speaking the promises of God over your life during times of weariness and exhaustion help you to be a winner in life. How?

13. When Jesus was on the Cross, He was thinking of others instead of His great pain. He gave sacrificially and unselfishly. Describe a time when you gave sacrificially and unselfishly.

14. God never wastes your pain. How will you challenge yourself to do good when feeling your worst?

15. Have the pressures you've faced in life forced you to become something other than what God has called you to be? Explain.

16. Christians are under pressure to stop believing in the Bible, marriage, hell, judgment, and in the sanctity of life. What do you think Jesus meant when he said, "for I always do those things that please Him," (John 8:29)?

17. Jesus continued doing good and giving His best in the face of harassments and accusations and He didn't change his course. How was Jesus able to do this?

18. Jesus never stopped being Christ. Have you ever been tempted to stop being a Christian? Explain.

Chapter 2

1. Do you believe that you can draw closer to Jesus by mastering spiritual disciplines? How?

2. What do you think David Livingston meant when he said, "I'll do anything as long as it's forward"?

3. Is it easier to overlook obstacles to appease your flesh as opposed to obstacles relating to your faith? Why? Name some vital spiritual disciplines that draw you closer to God.

4. True or False: A perfect situation and environment is needed to grow and give our best. Explain.

5. The New Testament tells us that Jesus was diverted and interrupted by people like Bartimaeus. When your time is interrupted are you able to give joyfully? Explain.

6. Give an example when you were interrupted and diverted. How did you handle the situation?

7. Was there ever a time in your life that you faced criticism for doing good? If so, explain.

8. What did Jesus do when He was criticized by the high priest?

9. Have you experienced betrayal and abandonment? How did it affect you and what did you do as a result of it?

10. Jesus constantly dealt with tension and undercurrents. How did he handle them? How does His example help you?

11. Can you recall a time in your life when tests and trials came and Jesus' example helped you through it? Explain.

12. Is it possible to rebound from failures? Why?

13. What does the saying, "be tougher than your toughest day" mean?

Chapter 3

1. Name a few things we, as Christians, don't have the right to do.

2. What is the reward for avoiding discord and doing good?

3. What protocol did Jesus give the disciples when he sent them out?

4. What must we do to protect our hearts against the few "bad apples" we will encounter through our lives?

5. When you have gone through all the necessary "steps" but things don't turn out the way you hoped. What must you do to stay on track?

6. Jesus never depended on his friends, followers, miracles or his treasury. Who do you think He depended on? Why?

7. A person, who doesn't have time to envy others, is a person who keeps himself _____.

8. How did Jesus prepare himself for the worst case scenario?

9. What should you do when pain is trying to control and dictate to your feelings?

10. How important is it to have the right perspective? Why?

11. What kind of seeds are you planting and what do you expect to reap?

12. Is your behavior starting to reshape your personality with excuses, complaining, and blaming? Explain.

13. Do you believe it would be helpful to interact with people you know during difficult times to encourage and strengthen you?

14. Do you agree with the statement that "we can't go through difficulties alone"? Why or why not?

15. People who have experienced a "major crises" and survived all have similar traits in common. A strong will to live and to do whatever it took to live. Have you ever experienced a major crisis and did your "will" play a major part surviving this experience? Explain.

16. Your will is the choice you make and no one but you can control your will. Do you agree or disagree with this statement? Why?

17. How important is it to visualize, and use your imagination in a good way, when you are making future plans for your life?

18. Do you think visualing and seeing yourself overcoming negative behaviors and thoughts is a good practice? Explain.

19. John 14:26 says the Holy Spirit is our Helper and Teacher. How important is it for us to go directly to the Holy Spirit when we are in need of help? Explain.

20. Do you think the Holy Spirit is the perfect coach? Why or why not?

21. Do you believe that it's important to be honest with oneself, if change is going to happen in a person's life?

22. Why do you think the Bible tells us to examine ourselves to see whether we are in faith?

23. Do you believe that our lives are for His service, His purpose and His glory? Would you say that you are currently living in obedience and honoring Him?

24. The What Would Jesus Do tattoo was a pretty good slogan to live by in the 90's. Do you believe it's still a good standard to live by today? Why or why not?

25. Do you think the persistence to do what's right will wear down the resistance of those who oppose and hinder you? Why or why not?

26. Do you believe the Holy Spirit will give you the persistence you need to do good, and give your best even though you fail and feel your worst? How?

27. Do you have a tendency to be impatient? What do you think your impatience is creating in your life?

28. Hebrews 6:12 says, "that you do not become sluggish, but imitate those who through faith and patience inherit the promises." What promises is this verse talking about?

29. Obedience is *"to hear God's Word and act accordingly."* Ask yourself, do you have a tendency to act according to God's Word or the opposite? Explain.

30. Do you believe that Jesus alone is a good motivation to act in obedience to the Word of God?

Chapter 4

1. Why is it important to teach our children the principle of Doing Good when they are young?

2. Are you willing to go and fulfill your purpose or would you rather remain silent? What ideas has God given you to bring this to pass in your life?

SCRIPTURES FOR DOING GOOD

Psalm 34:12-16 – Who is the man who desires life, and loves many days, that he may see good? Keep your tongue from evil, and your lips from speaking deceit. Depart from evil and do good; seek peace and pursue it.

Psalm 37:3 – Trust in the LORD, and do good; dwell in the land, and feed on His faithfulness.

Psalm 119:68 – You are good, and do good; teach me Your statutes.

Proverbs 3:27 – Do not withhold good from those to whom it is due, when it is in the power of your hand to do so.

Proverbs 31:12 – She does him good and not evil; all the days of her life.

Ecclesiastes 3:12 – I know that nothing is better for them than to rejoice, and to do good in their lives.

Micah 6:8 – He has shown you, O man, what is good; and what does the LORD require of you; but to do justly, to love mercy, and to walk humbly with your God?

Matthew 5:16 – Let your light so shine before men, that they may see your good works and glorify your Father in heaven.

Matthew 5:44 – But I say to you, love your enemies, bless those who curse you, do good to those who hate you, and pray for those who spitefully use you and persecute you.

Acts 9:36 – At Joppa there was a certain disciple named Tabitha, which is translated Dorcas. This woman was full of good works and charitable deeds which she did.

2 Corinthians 9:8 – And God is able to make all grace abound toward you, that you, always having all sufficiency in all things, may have an abundance for every good work.

Galatians 6:9-10 – And let us not grow weary while doing good, for in due season we shall reap if we do not lose heart. Therefore, as we have opportunity, let us do good to all, especially to those who are of the household of faith.

Ephesians 2:10 – For we are His workmanship, created in Christ Jesus for good works, which God prepared beforehand that we should walk in them.

Ephesians 4:28 – Let him who stole steal no longer, but rather let him labor, working with his hands what is good, that he may have something to give him who has need.

Scriptures for Doing Good

Ephesians 4:31-32 – Let all bitterness, wrath, anger, clamor, and evil speaking be put away from you, with all malice. And be kind to one another, tenderhearted, forgiving one another, even as God in Christ forgave you.

Philipians 2:4 – Let each of you look out not only for his own interests, but also for the interests of others.

Philippians 2:12-13 – Therefore, my beloved, as you have always obeyed, not as in my presence only, but now much more in my absence, work out your own salvation with fear and trembling; for it is God who works in you both to will and to do for His good pleasure.

Colossians 1:10-12 – that you may walk worthy of the Lord, fully pleasing Him, being fruitful in every good work and increasing in the knowledge of God; strengthened with all might, according to His glorious power, for all patience and longsuffering with joy; giving thanks to the Father who has qualified us to be partakers of the inheritance of the saints in the light.

Colossians 3:17 – And whatever you do, in word or deed, do everything in the name of the Lord Jesus, giving thanks to God the Father through him.

Colossians 3:23 – Whatever you do, work heartily, as for the Lord and not for men.

1 Thessalonians 5:15 – See that no one renders evil for evil to anyone, but always pursue what is good both for yourselves and for all.

1 Timothy 2:10 – But, which is proper for women professing godliness, with good works.

1 Timothy 5:10 – Well reported for good works: if she has brought up children, if she has lodged strangers, if she has relieved the afflicted, if she has deligently followed every good work.

2 Timothy 3:16 – All Scripture is given by inspiration of God, and is profitable for doctrine, for reproof, for correction, for instruction in righteousness, that the man of God may be complete, thoroughly equipped for every good work.

Titus 2:14 – Who gave Himself for us, that He might redeem us from every lawless deed and purify for Himself His own special people, zealous for good works.

Titus 3:14 –And let our people also learn to maintain good works, to meet urgent needs, that they may not be unfruitful.

1 Peter 3:10-12 – He who would love life and see good days, let him refrain his tongue from evil, and his lips from speaking deceit. Let him turn away from evil and do good; let him seek peace and pursue it. For the eyes of the LORD are on the righteous, and His ears are open to their prayers; but the face of the LORD is against those who do evil."

Scriptures for Doing Good

1 Peter 2:13-15 – Therefore submit yourselves to every ordinance of man for the Lord's sake, whether to the king as supreme, or to governors, as to those who are sent by him for the punishment of evildoers and for the praise of those who do good. For this is the will of God, that by doing good you may put to silence the ignorance of foolish men.

1 Peter 3:17 – For it is better, if it is the will of God, to suffer for doing good than for doing evil.

1 Peter 4:9 – Be hospitable to one another without grumbling.

Hebrews 6:10 – For God is not unjust to forget your work and labor of love which you have shown toward His name, in that you have ministered to the saints, and do minister.

SCRIPTURES FOR GIVING YOUR BEST

Genesis 24:19-20 – And when she had finished giving him a drink, she said, "I will draw water for your camels also, until they have finished drinking." Then she quickly emptied her pitcher into the trough, ran back to the well to draw water, and drew for all his camels.

Genesis 18:2-5 – So he lifted his eyes and looked, and behold, three men were standing by him; and when he saw them, he ran from the tent door to meet them, and bowed himself to the ground, and said, "My Lord, if I have now found favor in Your sight, do not pass on by Your servant. Please let a little water be brought, and wash your feet, and rest yourselves under the tree. And I will bring a morsel of bread, that you may refresh your hearts. After that you may pass by, inasmuch as you have come to your servant." They said, "Do as you have said."

Genesis 40:14 – But remember me when it is well with you, and please show kindness to me; make mention of me to Pharaoh, and get me out of this house.

Exodus 17:12 – But Moses' hands became heavy; so they took a stone and put it under him, and he sat on it. And Aaron and Hur supported his hands, one on one side, and the other on the other side; and his hands were steady until the going down of the sun.

Exodus 36:5 – And they spoke to Moses, saying, "The people bring much more than enough for the service of the work which the LORD commanded us to do."

Deuteronomy 15:11 – There will always be poor people in the land. Therefore I command you to be openhanded toward your fellow Israelites who are poor and needy in your land.

2 Kings 12:2 – Jehoash did what was right in the sight of the LORD all the days in which Jehoiada the priest instructed him.

Joshua 2:12 – Now therefore, I beg you, swear to me by the LORD, since I have shown you kindness, that you also will show kindness to my father's house, and give me a true token.

1 Chronicles 29:3 – Moreover, because I have set my affection on the house of my God, I have given to the house of my God, over and above all that I have prepared for the holy house, my own special treasure of gold and silver.

Proverbs 22:9 – He who has a generous eye will be blessed, for he gives of his bread to the poor.

Matthew 5:41-42 – And whoever compels you to go one mile, go with him two. Give to him who asks you, and from him who wants to borrow from you do not turn away.

Matthew 10:8 – Heal the sick, cleanse the lepers, raise the dead, cast out demons. Freely you have received, freely give.

Matthew 14:20 – So they all ate and were filled, and they took up twelve baskets full of the fragments that remained.

Matthew 18:22 – Jesus said to him, "I do not say to you, up to seven times, but up to seventy times seven."

Matthew 25:44-45 – "Then they also will answer Him, saying, 'Lord, when did we see You hungry or thirsty or a stranger or naked or sick or in prison, and did not minister to You?' Then He will answer them, saying, 'Assuredly, I say to you, inasmuch as you did not do it to one of the least of these, you did not do it to Me.'"

Luke 3:10-11 – So the people asked him, saying, "What shall we do then?" He answered and said to them, "He who has two tunics, let him give to him who has none; and he who has food, let him do likewise."

Luke 6:38 – Give, and it will be given to you: good measure, pressed down, shaken together, and running over will be put into your bosom. For with the same measure that you use, it will be measured back to you."

Luke 10:33-35 – But a certain Samaritan, as he journeyed, came where he was. And when he saw him, he had compassion. So he went to him and bandaged his wounds, pouring on oil and wine; and he set him on his own animal, brought him to an inn, and took care of him. On the next day, when he departed, he took out two denarii, gave them to the innkeeper, and said to him, "Take care of him; and whatever more you spend, when I come again, I will repay you."

Luke 21:3-4 – So He said, "Truly I say to you that this poor widow has put in more than all; for all these out of their abundance have put in offerings for God, but she out of her poverty put in all the livelihood that she had."

Luke 7:37-38 – And behold, a woman in the city who was a sinner, when she knew that Jesus sat at the table in the Pharisee's house, brought an alabaster flask of fragrant oil, and stood at His feet behind Him weeping; and she began to wash His feet with her tears, and wiped them with the hair of her head; and she kissed His feet and anointed them with the fragrant oil.

Luke 7:45 – "You gave Me no kiss, but this woman has not ceased to kiss My feet since the time I came in."

Romans 12:13 – Distributing to the needs of the saints, given to hospitality.

Titus 1:8 – But hospitable, a lover of what is good, sober-minded, just, holy, self-controlled.

Hebrews 13:2 – Do not forget to entertain strangers, for by so doing some have unwittingly enterained angels.

Hebrews 13:16 – But do not forget to do good and to share, for with such sacrifices God is well pleased.

James 2:14-17 – What does it profit, my brethren, if someone says he has faith but does not have works? Can faith save him? If a brother or sister is naked and destitute of daily food, and one of you says to them, "Depart in peace, be warmed and filled," but you do not give them the things which are needed for the body, what does it profit? Thus also faith by itself, if it does not have works, is dead.

James 3:13 – Who is wise and understanding among you? Let him show by good conduct that his works are done in the meekness of wisdom.

James 4:17 – Therefore, to him who knows to do good and does not do it, to him it is sin.